PopularMechanics

WHO'S SPYING ON YOU?

PopularMechanics

WHO'S SPYING ON YOU?

THE LOOMING THREAT TO YOUR PRIVACY, IDENTITY, AND FAMILY IN THE DIGITAL AGE

Erik Sofge and Davin Coburn

HEARST BOOKS
New York

HEARST BOOKS
New York

An Imprint of Sterling Publishing
387 Park Avenue South
New York, NY 10016

Popular Mechanics is a registered trademark of Hearst Communications, Inc.

Design by Jon Chaiet
Cover Image: Burcu Avsar

ISBN 978-1-58816-858-0

Library of Congress Cataloging-in-Publication Data

Sofge, Erik.
Popular mechanics who's spying on you? : the looming threat to your privacy, identity, and family in the digital age / Erik Sofge, Davin Coburn and the editors of Popular Mechanics.
p. cm.
ISBN 978-1-58816-858-0
1. Electronic surveillance. 2. Privacy, Right of. 3. Data protection. 4. Computer security. 5. Identity theft. I. Coburn, Davin. II. Popular mechanics (Chicago, Ill. : 1959) III. Title. IV. Title: Who's spying on you?
TK7882.E2S64 2012
613.6--dc23
2012015960

Distributed in Canada by Sterling Publishing
c/o Canadian Manda Group, 165 Dufferin Street
Toronto, Ontario, Canada M6K 3H6

Distributed in the United Kingdom by GMC Distribution Services
Castle Place, 166 High Street, Lewes, East Sussex, England BN7 1XU

Distributed in Australia by Capricorn Link (Australia) Pty. Ltd.
P.O. Box 704, Windsor, NSW 2756, Australia

For information about custom editions, special sales, and premium and corporate purchases, please contact Sterling Special Sales at 800-805-5489 or specialsales@sterlingpublishing.com.

Manufactured in the United States of America

2 4 6 8 10 9 7 5 3 1

www.sterlingpublishing.com

TABLE OF CONTENTS

CHAPTER 1

WHO'S SPYING ON YOU

PRIVACY IS ANCIENT. It's as old as human life, born in the earliest whispers, stitched into the first clothes. It's a concept so primal that any attempt to define it, by dragging it through the nebbish taxonomies of academia and law, drains its vital meaning. We instinctually know what privacy is. It's about identity and ideas that thrive in isolation, and what withers when scrutinized. It's the darkroom that's dark for a reason.

The *right* to privacy, though, is a highly modern concept. The term is usually traced backed to 1890, as the title of a paper published in the *Harvard Law Review*. The authors, Samuel Warren and Louis Brandeis, were partners at a new Boston law firm, and had become alarmed at the sudden intersection of two powerful technologies: the newspaper printing press, capable of ever bigger and faster print runs, and the Kodak, a portable, fast-shooting camera that enabled, for the first time in history, candid shots of unsuspecting subjects. "Instantaneous photographs and newspaper enterprise have invaded the sacred precincts of private and domestic life; and numerous mechanical devices threaten to make good the prediction that "what is whispered in the closet shall be proclaimed from the house-tops,' " wrote Warren and Brandeis. That was their short-term fear—that gossip would become contagious and all-consuming, and no longer an occupational hazard reserved for public figures. They also worried, upstanding 19th century gentlemen that they were, about the honor of women, that their portraits would be taken at random and "colored to suit a gross and depraved imagination."

At that time, two years into the release of the Kodak, amateur photography was transforming American culture. Most cameras still used wet film plates, which had to be dipped and loaded into bulky, hooded contraptions. The Kodak was six and a half inches long, and came preloaded with enough dry plate film for 100 shots. The whole thing could be shipped back to the company, and the developed film and reloaded camera would then be returned to the owner. Despite a steep price tag— $25, or roughly $600 adjusting for inflation—thousands of the cameras had been sold by 1890. Reports of scoundrels sneaking photos of women in bathing suits led to posted warnings at beaches, and at least one resort banned the camera altogether. To some, this was a frightening, destabilizing moment. Technology was outpacing society, and possibly the law.

What started as a quaintly pre-information age defense of collective propriety quickly turns spooky. They were concerned that everything would eventually be recorded and distributed at will. Warren and Brandeis effectively vault over Perez and Paris Hilton to a future where privacy is at the mercy of technology. The gadgets, they argued, were the key. They captured and disseminated. Identities that had always flowed in and out of public spaces could now be bottled, and sold.

Warren and Brandeis saw a way out. They claimed that, buried within legal precedents, somewhere between the hard losses of stolen property and the softer, but widely recognized impact of mental anguish, was a principle that protected privacy. Cases that punished the theft of intellectual property and trade secrets, they wrote, "indicate a general right to privacy for thoughts, emotions, and sensations." Privacy is hard to pin down, and impossible to quantify, but should be as protected as anything else we own, "whether expressed in writing, or in conduct, in conversation, in attitudes, or in facial expression."

The "Right to Privacy" would be heralded as one of the most important legal articles in history. While Warren eventually quit practicing law, Louis Brandeis went on to become a United States Supreme Court Justice. The Kodak sold unabated, and paved the way for the Kodak-Eastman film camera, and countless iterations of devices that record the sights and sounds of public life. And somewhere along the line, all of Warren and Brandeis's nightmares came true.

GONE IN THE BLINK OF A SHUTTER

It took years, more than a hundred of them, but the invasion is complete. Cameras have taken up position throughout the modern world, and they continue to propagate. There are more than 30 million surveillance cameras in the United States today. They record the daily movements of pedestrians. They snap pictures of cars speeding or blowing red lights. Bolted to the roofs of Google's StreetView vehicles, 360-degree camera arrays take in whole neighborhoods. The cameras appear without warning or consent. Whatever broad protections Warren and Brandeis were championing never materialized. In the 21st century, much like the 19th century, there is no privacy in public.

This isn't a loophole. The patchwork of laws that govern privacy in the U.S. all hinge on a central concept: the reasonable expectation of privacy. In the home, that expectation nears 100 percent. If a person peers through the window, or aims or plants a camera inside, they're subject to a litany of criminal and civil punishments. But the moment someone exits his or her home, that expectation collapses, and privacy begins to dissipate.

BUT THE MOMENT SOMEONE EXITS HIS OR HER HOME, EXPECTATION COLLAPSES, AND PRIVACY BEGINS TO DISSIPATE.

In fact, only the naive would expect anything less than constant visual surveillance. This is the most familiar and, for some, the most hopeless front in the ongoing assault on privacy. It's a battle that was lost decades ago. The cameras are an ugly, inescapable fact of life. Bringing them up marks you as a nag, the type of person who worries about the millions of germs lurking on every door handle. Or worse, someone who trolls online forums for the latest rumors of bizarre surveillance breakthroughs, systems that are stranger than science fiction. Rumors like these:

■ Security cameras are more than cameras—they're robots. Or the eyes and ears, really, of a new generation of machines that surveil their terrain with a hive-mind intelligence. Instead of one person watching banks of display monitors, networked security systems now watch themselves, the software picking suspicious targets out of crowds based on erratic movements, elevated body temperature, and various other criteria. "Our experience shows automating camera monitoring can make human monitoring completely redundant," Robert Allen of Abeo Technical Solutions told Popular Mechanics. Abeo's AWARE system (Automated Warning And Response Engine) has been installed in airports around the country, where it watches for specific behavior—subjects lingering in a given area, or passing the wrong way through a gate. Allen claimed that, because of the system's ability to make decisions, a few human operators can manage thousands of feeds. This field is called video analytics, and it's not science fiction anymore. From cutting-edge casinos to retail clothing chains, the cameras are thinking, in their limited way, about whom to watch, and why.

■ Our faces are being recorded, and filed away for later use. While attempts by law enforcement to set up national and even international catalogs of faces have been largely shouted down, the commercial sector has been creating its own databases of facial images for years. Surveillance systems can now automatically detect and store faces, and attach a variety of data to them. At the Redner's Markets chain of grocery and convenience stores on the East Coast, the faces of known thieves are tagged, and will trigger an alert as soon as they show up on camera at any of the store locations. Criminals aren't the cameras' only targets, however. Starting in 2008, T-Mobile began collecting the faces of customers at its stores, in the hopes of tracking fraudulent transactions. That meant pairing specific faces with specific purchases, part of a growing, searchable database. Merging facial recognition with more traditional video analytics, T-Mobile hopes to track which customers are looking at which devices, for how long, and when that browsing results in an actual sale.

■ Computers know a liar when they see one. At the University of Arizona, researchers have developed an interactive kiosk, called Avatar, to interrogate human subjects at airports and border crossings. As the on-screen, computer-generated avatar runs through typical security screener questions, a suite of sensors watches for 15 different "lying cues." A camera tracks face and body movements, while an infrared sensor gauges millimeter-length twitches in pupil size, as well as changes in skin temperature. The subject's voice is analyzed, too, for abnormal modulation. No tell is too small, and Avatar's creators—who are part of a Transportation Security Administration-funded center at the university—claim that the fully autonomous system beats its human counterparts at catching suspicious behavior. When that happens, Avatar declares: "I am detecting deception in your responses." The session may continue, but the machine has already made up its mind.

Clearly, the cameras aren't done with us yet. Watching the population was once a linear, manpower-intensive activity, forcing law enforcement, private businesses or whoever else had an interest in surveillance to narrow their field of view, focusing on specific areas, individuals and stretches of time. Installing more cameras meant hiring more eyeballs to watch video monitors live, or slog through reels or tapes after the fact. Even when digital cameras drove down the cost of hardware and storage, allowing for exponentially more cameras and footage, the humans were still the bottleneck in the system. It wasn't until the late 1990s and early 2000s that we began to treat the images collected by cameras not as footage, but as data.

What's the difference? Footage acts like a ribbon, unspooling in one direction or the other, allowing itself to be sliced apart and spliced back together, but always ultimately linear. It has to be monitored. Data is much stranger, and more malleable. It can be ground into individual bits and reassembled into new shapes and functions. It can also be merged with other data, into databases that are almost instantly searched and reorganized. Facial features that drift into frame are mapped and bundled into datasets. Those faces can then be tied to names, credit histories and criminal records. Data doesn't need to be watched—it watches itself. When the goal is to analyze the activities of huge numbers of people, data is more powerful than footage has ever been.

Unfortunately, data is also promiscuous. It can be reused—captured for one purpose, such as T-Mobile's fraud prevention effort, then funneled into a broader plan to put a face to every sale in a given store, and marry facial features with sensitive financial information. That particular plan may have been a limited pilot, but the practice of reusing facial databases has already gone national. Starting in 2009, the FBI began using facial recognition software to scour the driver's license photos taken by the DMV, searching for features that match those of known fugitives. This is a prelude, of sorts, to the agency's own long-term plans to set up a database of various uniquely identifiable markers. The Next Generation Identification System will eventually include facial features, iris scans, and possibly even records of a subject's gait, or how he or she walks. The FBI resists claims that the project is a mass identification program. "We aren't going to start collecting irises from everyone and their brother," said Thomas Bush, who served as assistant director of the FBI's Criminal Justice Information Services Division until March 2009. "We adhere to very strict privacy guidelines. We're taking more biometrics from the same people we were always authorized to take fingerprints from."

> STARTING IN 2009, THE FBI BEGAN USING FACIAL RECOGNITION SOFTWARE TO SCOUR THE DRIVER'S LICENSE PHOTOS TAKEN BY THE DMV, SEARCHING FOR FEATURES THAT MATCH THOSE OF KNOWN FUGITIVES.

FOCUSING ON SECURITY

Worries over ever-greater camera presence in our lives can be something of a Rorschach test: Are the hundreds of body scanners showing up in airport security lines nationwide a long-overdue burst of innovation, or the onset of a surveillance state? Is it comforting or troubling that officers in the Pinella's County Sherriff's Office in Florida take digital photos of subjects in the field, and then run those images, on the spot, for a potential match against a collection of 5 million facial profiles? Or that the makers of that system, L-1 Identity Solutions, also recommend using face-matching to help identify sketches of suspects? In each case, the potential for abuse seems undeniable, but for now it's largely only potential. Weighed against the possibility of letting a violent criminal slip away because of a fake ID, or an airline passenger smuggle a loaded handgun onto a plane—as a flier in Detroit was caught attempting in December 2011—vague protests over privacy implications don't stand a chance.

This is the real legacy of the cameras. They set a concrete precedent for the surrender of privacy in exchange for security. After all, surveillance cameras became inexpensive for lots of reasons, but ubiquitous for one: safety. Every so often, lightning strikes—the lens finds an armed robber, a child abductor, or a cell of terrorists. Critics of London's comprehensive network of more than a million cameras (the highest concentration in the world) lost all traction after a series of bombs ripped through the city in 2005. Weeks of scanning footage finally led to the capture of the rest of the cell, a process that video analytics firms say could have been cut down to days using visual search algorithms.

According to privacy experts, though, the London bombings were a rare win for the cameras. On every day that lightning doesn't strike, these devices surveil ordinary people living their increasingly recorded lives. Studies of police cameras in Los Angeles, San Francisco, and London have shown that the presence of surveillance cameras has no impact on violent crime. In Chicago, many of the cameras installed in recent years have broken down, including one that overlooked the beating death of a high school honor student in 2009. Still, more closed-circuit cameras are going up in cities across the United States. And back in the United Kingdom, the cameras are on the move—police are using unmanned aerial vehicles to conduct air patrols. These quadcopter drones can be piloted remotely, but they also operate autonomously, navigating their way along preset routes, scanning the streets below with heat-sensitive infrared cameras.

In a moment of existential panic, it's easy to put all of these pieces together a little too neatly. The FBI doesn't have access to T-Mobile's facial database. Loan officers aren't using advanced analytics to compare applicant photos with a national index of police sketches. The TSA's Avatar, for all its uncanny powers of deduction, isn't distributing a list of known liars to the highest bidders.

For now, all of these systems are fragmented. But how long will that last? "What happens when a tabloid buys a drone and says, 'Here's a picture of Brad Pitt,'" says Ryan Calo, Director of the Consumer Privacy Project at Stanford Law School, "'now go fly around LA and find him, and 10 other celebrities like him'?" The Federal Aviation Administration currently restricts that kind of activity, and even grounded the LA Country Sheriff's Department's plans to field its own drone. But as Calo points out, laws change quickly. Just as today's paparazzi are free to swarm celebrities, and police helicopters are cleared to thunder over inner cities, tomorrow's privacy reality could include flocks of robots in a constant, unyielding overflight of public spaces.

If that sounds ludicrous, imagine what Warren and Brandeis would think of the millions of cameras currently perched around the world. Threats to privacy evolve quickly, cycling rapid-fire through generations like a colonizing bacteria. Just as Warren and Brandis worried about the popularity of the Kodak, and its convergence with newspapers, today's experts are anxiously tracking the birth of true facial recognition, which could impact nearly every aspect of camera-based surveillance.

Forget those swarming robots for a moment (if you can). Apple, Google, and Facebook have all rolled out limited facial recognition features, allowing users to tag a given face in a photo, and then search through their own photos for likely matches. And, in perhaps the most harrowing day-to-day application of this technology, some researchers are using similar off-the-shelf technology to search far more than their own hard drives: At the Black Hat security conference in Las Vegas last summer, Alessandro Acquisti, an associate professor of information technology and public policy at Carnegie Mellon University, presented the results of a study he conducted with a pair of CMU postdoctoral fellows, Ralph Gross and Fred Stutzman. The research team combined three off-the-shelf modern technologies—the PittPatt face recognizing program, "cloud" computing and publicly available information from social network sites—to snap photos of complete strangers, then track down the subjects' real identities by scouring the Internet for a facial match.

APPLE, GOOGLE AND FACEBOOK HAVE ALL ROLLED OUT LIMITED FACIAL RECOGNITION FEATURES, ALLOWING USERS TO TAG A GIVEN FACE IN A PHOTO, AND THEN SEARCH THROUGH THEIR OWN PHOTOS FOR LIKELY MATCHES.

Similar, rudimentary matching technology has been around for decades—but its ultimate effectiveness has long been constrained by the number of reference photos in the user's database. In 2001, for instance, authorities in Tampa, Florida, took clandestine photos of 72,000 fans passing through the turnstiles at the Super Bowl—though their limited database only connected 19 to minor criminal backgrounds. But by searching the entire cloud—in essence, the massive trove of information underpinning the Internet—Carnegie Mellon's database became nearly infinite.

In one experiment, the team identified the full names of unknown students based on their Facebook profiles, in about a minute—something of an unsettling party trick. In another example, the team sleuthed out the real names of individuals on a popular online dating site where members use pseudonyms—a frighteningly personal step that could present real-world safety concerns. Acquisti's team's third experiment, however, is the truly terrifying one: In 2009, Acquisti and Gross had studied the assignment scheme of Social Security numbers (SSNs)—and discovered that an individual's SSN can be predicted with surprising accuracy entirely from public data. Using special algorithms they developed, "we found that it [was] possible to combine information from government sources with simple demographic data [such as an individual's state and date of birth, widely available from commercial databases, voter registration lists, or online social networks] to predict narrow ranges of values wherein individual SSNs are likely to fall," the team wrote. Combining that with the technology in the 2011 study, a photo led to an identity, the cloud provided public data—and soon the team at Carnegie Mellon was looking at strangers' Social Security numbers.

Acquisti's *coup de grâce? He made it mobile:* The researchers built a smartphone application to demonstrate the ability of making the same sensitive inferences in real-time. In an example of "augmented reality," as they called it, the team's application uses the phone's camera and Internet connection to overlay personal and private information over the target's face on the smartphone's screen. "Ultimately, all this access is going to force us to reconsider our notions of privacy," Acquisti said. "It may also affect how we interact with each other. Through natural evolution, human beings have evolved mechanisms to assign and manage trust in face-to-face interactions. Will we rely on our instincts or on our devices, when mobile phones can predict personal and sensitive information about a person?"

For now, the unwashed masses can't search all of Facebook, or the entire Internet, for a specific face. (Acquisti says the idea of selling his app or letting it into the public domain horrifies him.) But in both cases, the core technology is already up and running; the only question is who has access to the algorithms. Soon after this book hits the shelves, free, comprehensive facial recognition might be as commonplace as Googling a stranger's address, and zooming in on their front yard with Street View. Once that happens, facial recognition would be as ubiquitous as cameras, and picking faces out of video wouldn't be far behind. "We have an expectation of anonymity in public," says Beth Givens, Director of the Privacy Rights Clearinghouse. "You know you're being watched, but you're not being identified. When you combine video surveillance in public places with biometric facial recognition, then we're in trouble. It has the potential to become the ultimate privacy disaster."

Of course, there's no such thing as Google Face or Facebook Look-Book. You can't type in someone's name and watch that person stumbling out of a strip club, or walking into an abortion clinic, or protesting at a rally yet. For that to happen, nothing new would have to invented. The cameras are already in place, and packed with machine intelligence. The networks are built and optimized. The code is written. All it would take is for someone to decide it's worth the risk. Maybe the system would catch some criminals. Or better yet, a terrorist. Almost any excuse would do.

IN THE WAR FOR AND AGAINST PRIVACY, THE CAMERAS WILL ALWAYS WIN.

In the war for and against privacy, the cameras will always win. They simply promise too much. But there are more fronts in this fight. Not all of them are lost.

CHAPTER 2

WHO'S SPYING ON YOUR LOCATION

OF ALL THE MYTHS HOLLYWOOD HAS GIVEN US, few are as consistently silly as the tracking device. They always blink, and often beep, and tend to transmit their location as handy little blips, sliding in real-time across computer monitors. These cartoonish doodads, lurking under cars or in the guts of electronics, are such common plot devices they don't even have to be explained. They emit radiowaves, maybe. There's probably a battery onboard. And until someone discovers the tracker and stomps it to pieces, someone else is diligently watching that blip's progress. That the best minds in Cold War espionage never came up with a real-world device that even resembled these elegant gadgets is beside the point. What makes this vision of privacy invasion so ludicrous is that it's so intimate. Someone has to tiptoe into position to plant the tracker. Then, a whole team of caffeinated desk jockeys is on rotating blip duty. Almost no one's movements are worth that amount of effort, or overtime.

In recent years, however, a new plot device has shown up on the big and small screen. Now, Big Brother can pinpoint a target's location through a standard mobile phone, either zeroing in on the cellular connection, or hijacking the GPS signal. These are clear-cut plot devices, but the implication is sobering—the phones we all carry are a button-push away from betraying us.

If only the screenwriters were making it up. In fact, they might be downplaying the current state of location tracking. The typical mobile phone is now a full-service tracking device, whose basic operation requires that it announce its position in the world on a constant basis. To ensure stable, persistent cell service and an efficient flow of data for every customer in a provider's network, cellphones regularly power up and ping nearby cellular towers. Individual connections are handed off to whichever tower is sending it the strongest signal, a process that helps avoid bandwidth traffic jams, and allows for a loose sort of triangulation of a phone's location.

The technique known as tower triangulation—where overlapping rings of coverage from every tower in range create a kind of Venn diagram, narrowing the phone's location down to somewhere within those intersecting bands—wasn't cooked up by nosy mobile providers. It was a response to a long-running federal initiative to give emergency responders the precise location of a victim calling for help. When every phone was a landline tied to a listed physical address, complying with Enhanced 911, or E911, was simple. The mobile phone demands more innovation. "Part of the reason cell phones are so good at getting a precise location is the E911 mandate," says Jim Harper, Director of Information Policy Studies at the Cato Institute. "The cell companies were required to get good at triangulating, really fast." By building a running record of a phone's probable locations, and analyzing how fast it traveled between coverage cells, as well as the peaks and valleys of its fluctuating signal strength during each ping, providers are able to triangulate to within 1000 yards of a handset's current location. Once GPS chips became common in mobile phones, the E911 mandated kicked in once more, forcing providers to increase the accuracy of their tracking of GPS-enabled devices. The blip shrank from a sloppy, 1000-yard "maybe" to a true pinprick on a map, with an accuracy of just over 2 yards when GPS signals are unobstructed and at their strongest.

MORE INSIDIOUSLY, RESEARCHERS RECENTLY DISCOVERED THAT MANY MOBILE PHONES BUILD DATABASES OF THEIR USERS' WHEREABOUTS, A SNEAKY FEATURE THAT DOESN'T ASK FOR PERMISSION, OR REVEAL ITS EXISTENCE.

Like so many privacy threats, this one started out as an unabashed win for public security: A life-saving feature had bridged the wireless divide. And, as a fringe benefit, it enabled nifty apps that help you locate your misplaced phone.

Then came the reuse.

First, law enforcement piggy-backed onto the technology, demanding access to those databases of user locations with a subpoena—no warrant necessary. Private industry followed, with Google's ubiquitous Maps application, which has been feeding GPS-based tracking data to the developers of location-based iPhone applications since the second generation of the smartphone was released in 2008. In 2010, Blackberry-maker Research In Motion began providing its own developers with tower-triangulation data, which had traditionally been off-limits to the commercial sector. More insidiously, researchers recently discovered that many mobile phones build databases of their users' whereabouts, a sneaky feature that doesn't ask for permission, or reveal its existence.

In April 2011, Alasdair Allan, senior research fellow in astronomy at the University of Exeter, in the United Kingdom, and writer Pete Warden found the Apple's iOS4 operating system collected coordinates and timestamps for its phones and 3G iPads, then quietly copied the data to any computer the device synched with. The location history was unencrypted and unprotected—and theoretically available to anyone with access to your phone. "By passively logging your location without your permission," the duo wrote, "Apple have made it possible for anyone from a jealous spouse to a private investigator to get a detailed picture of your movements."

That discovery followed another eyebrow-raising development from the Cupertino company: Since 2008, device owners could find notice of Apple's potential intent to monitor location information buried at the end of various programs' End User License Agreements. But in June 2010, the company updated its general privacy policy and left no doubt: "To provide location-based services on Apple products, Apple and our partners and licensees may collect, use, and share precise location data, including the real-time geographic location of your Apple computer or device." That move prompted a letter to Steve Jobs from U.S. Reps. Edward Markey and Joe Barton noting, "Given the limited ability of Apple users to opt out of the revised policy and still be able to take advantage of the features of their Apple products, we are concerned about the impact the collection of such data could have on the privacy of Apple's customers."

Meanwhile, Android devices fared no better. Security analyst Samy Kamkar, who conducted research on the phones for the *Wall Street Journal*, found that, "An HTC Android phone collected its location every few seconds and transmitted the data to Google at least several times an hour. It also transmitted the name, location and signal strength of any nearby Wi-Fi networks, as well as a unique phone identifier."

In each of these instances, the trackers make assurances. Manufacturers claim they don't access the location data stored on their phones. Besides, they argue, smartphone owners want the capabilities that location data provides, often freely handing it over (usually by approving a pop-up window that asks for permission to use your location). For instance, Yelp, a clearinghouse for user-generated restaurant reviews and ratings, uses GPS and Google Maps to pinpoint your smartphone's location during the 10 minutes that you're tapping around for the nearest diner. The data flow dries up the moment you quit the application. And subpoenaed cell tower records are often considered something of an urban legend—in most cases, a phone's location history sits in a database for no longer than 24 hours before its overwritten. Unless you're the target of an active investigation, and have the constant attention of one or more agents reporting on your every cell phone ping, that threat is entirely hypothetical. So what if we paid for the tracking devices and planted them on our own persons? Lucky for us blips, we're told, no one is bored enough to watch a billion dots inching through the maze of everyday life.

E-Z TO TRACK: LEAVING FOOTPRINTS IN THE FAST LANE

It takes a leap of faith to find comfort in these caveats. First, you have to stop asking questions, such as why Apple or Google bothers collecting detailed information that it never uses, or where Yelp's logs of user locations are stored, and how securely? And while tower triangulation is more of a concern for suspects in the crosshairs of an FBI operation, what's to stop law enforcement agencies from picking through other databases of location data?

In fact, they've been doing exactly that for years. E-ZPass records, in particular, have been a powerful tool for the authorities. Each wireless handshake the transponder makes with a tollbooth leaves a data trail, time-stamping the user's presence. Investigators have used this location history to expose fraud, often in the form of bogus overtime claims. The most famous case, in 2003, led to the conviction or transfer of some thirty New York Police Department narcotics officers, when their E-ZPass accounts logged bridge and tunnel crossings during hours they had claimed were spent filling out post-arrest paperwork.

Within a few years of that case, however, the more widespread impact of location data reuse hit the courts, as divorce lawyers began presenting E-ZPass records as evidence of extramarital affairs. The damage was inflicted not by placing a suspected cheater in a specific, torrid meeting spot, but by catching **DIVORCE LAWYERS BEGAN PRESENTING E-ZPASS RECORDS AS EVIDENCE OF EXTRA-MARITAL AFFAIRS.** him or her in a lie. Though policies vary by state, in Maryland E-ZPass data are retained for 18 months, long enough to establish a pattern of suspicious travel, or simply pry into a year and a half of someone's life on the road.

Not surprisingly, the general public isn't exactly flying to the defense of the country's alleged cheaters. As location tracking comes of age, privacy experts worry about where the technology goes next. Tempting as it is to lump the morally bankrupt together with overtime scammers and dismiss them all, there's an important distinction. One group is the target of a criminal investigation, with the full weight of law enforcement behind it. The other group is part of a civil dispute. Yet, both are subject to the same retroactive surveillance technique, which reaches back through time, and turns an innocuous wireless payment gadget into something it was never intended to be: a makeshift tracking device.

This is where it gets scary, and too complex for Hollywood to fit into frame. The betrayals, by our phones, by our E-ZPass transponders, by the GPS chips in our cars and digital cameras, have already happened. These devices are all gushing location data, with varying degrees of accuracy or resolution, but the hemorrhage is ongoing. For now, the large-scale impact is in civil and criminal cases, affecting people who no one would accuse of being innocent bystanders. But with the increasing number of devices tracking us, it's only a matter of time before the kinds of data breaches that regularly expose customers' financial or medical information extend to the vast histories of physical locations. "I think there are going to be some data Valdeses around smartphones and location, if there haven't already been," says Beth Givens, director of the Privacy Rights Clearinghouse. As we'll see in later chapters, sensitive data is sometimes compromised without public awareness or apologies. Our information is gathered in silence, and sold, stolen or repurposed just as quietly.

One of the newest examples of stealthy location tracking is mounted on police cars across the country. Automatic license plate readers, specialized cameras that detect and capture still images of license plates, were designed to function as robotic wingmen. As a patrol vehicle cruises down a street full of parked cars, the reader runs every plate it sees, and sounds an alarm if an outstanding warrant or other report (stolen vehicle, missing persons, etc.) comes up. As data goes, the plate reader is an industrial vacuum, hoovering up as many as 900 plates per minute from up to 50 ft. away, and feeding them into a dedicated computer in the trunk. "The officer gets results in near real time," said PIPS' vice president of marketing, Brian Shockley, "or about 20 milliseconds." The most popular plate readers now incorporate geo-tagging, attaching GPS coordinates to each stored plate image, and building a running database of when and where each vehicle was located.

To be clear, plate readers don't simply retain records of suspicious vehicles, and dump the thousands of bystander plates they capture every day. Everything is saved. Law enforcement agencies tend to downplay this daily, nonstop cataloguing of vehicle locations. PIPS Technology, the leading manufacturer of automatic license plate readers, isn't as squeamish, touting as a selling point that detailed location histories could be analyzed by investigators after the fact. Plates spotted in the vicinity of a crime could yield witnesses, or suspects. One proposed application of plate readers makes location tracking the primary mission—PIPS has marketed its systems as discrete attachments to streetlights or other roadside elements, keeping tabs on vehicles that might later be tied to terrorist watch lists.

AS A PATROL VEHICLE CRUISES DOWN A STREET FULL OF PARKED CARS, THE READER RUNS EVERY PLATE IT SEES, AND SOUNDS AN ALARM IF AN OUTSTANDING WARRANT OR OTHER REPORT COMES UP.

This is a potential convergence of twin privacy threats: the wholesale collection of seemingly infinite amounts of personally identifiable data in a never-ending, automated dragnet (often summed up as mass surveillance), and the seemingly infinite reuse of that persistent influx of data. Neither the collection nor the reuse is illegal. But together, they exploit data's promiscuous side. Whether they're confirming a pop-up window on a smartphone, or bolting a unique proof of identity onto their vehicle, users consent to the initial use and storage of their information. This data is entrusted to another party, in exchange for access (to Yelp's own data, or to roads and highways). It flows further, though, spilling from servers after cyberattacks, or gathered by those plate readers. Data isn't loyal to its source. It would be useless if it weren't so pliable. Data must comply.

What's taking shape in location tracking is a dark and ubiquitous capacity. The data doesn't even have to be damning. Evidence of a suspect's vicinity to a crime could lead to a wrongful conviction. Unexplained detours could push a strained marriage toward collapse. Whatever the answers, the tracking will generate questions. When casual interrogations have to be deflected, and privacy has to be actively defended, much of the damage is already done.

Of course, carping on the dire future of mass data reuse can be another kind of assurance—there's a storm brewing, echoes of abuses to come if we don't act. But this isn't like the cameras. There's still time.

PRECISION-GUIDED MURDER

For James Harrison's children, it's far too late. In 2009, the diesel mechanic used a GPS tracking feature to locate his wife's cellphone. He found her at a convenience store with another man. They argued. He returned to their home in Pierce County, Washington. That night, Harrison shot all five of his children to death, and then himself.

Blaming GPS tracking for those murders is too tidy—according to police reports, James Harrison's 16-year-old daughter, Maxine, had helped her father use the tracking feature to locate her mother, and accompanied him to the convenience store confrontation. Did that single breach of privacy, not so much an act of high-tech stalking as another strange scene in an unfolding domestic tragedy, trigger the massacre? Or was Harrison's rampage a foregone conclusion, a matter of when, not if?

What's clear, though, is that location tracking is not a hypothetical threat to privacy—it's already impacting ordinary people, every day, across the country. In 2009, the Department of Justice estimated that some 25,000 adults were the victims of GPS stalking, a number that's bound to have climbed with the popularity of smartphones. Some cases involve optional features, activated as part of a cell provider's family plan. Others require the installation of surveillance software that feeds call logs, text messages and GPS data to the snooping client.

And then there's the direct approach, a tactic that seems too bizarre, like too much of a Hollywood invention, to be true. But in recent years, life has imitated art—the tracking device has arrived. Compared to their spy movie counterparts, they're graceless hunks of technology, bigger than a deck of cards, and designed almost exclusively to track vehicles.

Battery life is also an issue. The $400 SleuthGear PTX5, for example, runs for 8 hrs when reporting continuous, real-time GPS coordinates, or for 10 days when sending updates every 10 seconds. Planting these devices, then replanting fully-charged replacements, requires dedication.

IN 2009, THE DEPARTMENT OF JUSTICE ESTIMATED THAT SOME 25,000 ADULTS WERE THE VICTIMS OF GPS STALKING.

Their legality is also still up for debate. In Washington, D.C., the courts threw out a case against a suspected cocaine dealer, because police officers had tracked his vehicle without a warrant. In San Francisco, however, the 9th Circuit Court upheld the warrantless installation of a GPS tracker, despite the fact that officers attached it while the vehicle was parked in the suspect's private driveway. In his dissenting opinion, Judge Alex Kozinski claimed that this precedent gave "the government the power to track the movements of every one of us, every day of our lives." He added that "[the] needs of law enforcement, to which my colleagues seem inclined to refuse nothing, are quickly making personal privacy a distant memory. 1984 may have come a bit later than predicted, but it's here at last."

The U.S. Supreme Court is expected to weigh on the issue soon. That decision won't result in a ban on GPS tracking devices, though. And whatever happens, it'll be too little, and far too late for one more victim of the war on privacy.

In 2011, Jitka Vesel was leaving work, walking through the parking lot, when her ex-boyfriend opened fire. They had broken up years ago. A few days earlier he had glued a GPS tracker to her car. He had watched the blip's progress across his computer screen, in and around the Chicago area, until it came to rest in this suburb. Dmitry Smirnov had picked his killing field. He approached Vesel, and fired at least eleven rounds. She was pronounced dead at the scene.

CHAPTER 3

WHO'S SPYING ON YOUR HOME

THE MODERN AMERICAN HOME IS SEETHING WITH ENERGY. Not in the generic, Physics 101 sense, where excited particles churn out of furnaces, wander the house, and steal out through drafty windows. That's a prehistoric phenomenon, a constant since fire pits were moved indoors. This bloom of energy is newer, and travels further. If it were visible, it would turn suburban streets into a mass of luminous tentacles. City blocks would be even brighter, the frequencies blending into a uniform, blinding glow.

The energy is radio waves, and they pour out of houses and apartments and flood the outside world at a rate that climbs every year. Wireless routers broadcast past exterior walls, announce their availability, invade neighboring homes and beam invitations to passing smartphones. Smart utility meters push further still, in long, looping connections that funnel data to receivers miles away. In 2005 some 10 million U.S. homes had wireless internet access, and none had smart meters. Today, 30 million homes have a WiFi access point, and by 2015, an estimated 40 million homes could be equipped with smart meters.

On most days, in most places, that massive web of radio frequencies is simply an invisible latticework in the background. But what if a person could drag a net through that free-flying data, and filter out any information they wanted? With the right gear, and the proper training, the wrong sorts of people could sidestep centuries of legal protections that have made the home a bastion of privacy. Walls and doors mean nothing if the radio signals pass straight through.

In 2010, a team of researchers at the University of Virginia gave shape to that fear. After spending a week scanning the radio emissions at eight different kinds of homes, they were able to reconstruct the detailed living patterns of the occupants. They knew when the residents used front and back doors. They knew when they were away, and when they were asleep. That the researchers figured this out without aiming a single camera at their targets was impressive, but it doesn't take a post-graduate degree to visually case a potential victim's home. So they dug deeper, using a sophisticated computer algorithm to decode the scattered bursts of radio waves, guessing which frequencies were light sensors, and which might be thermostats. They called it a Fingerprint And Timing-based Snooping (FATS) attack, based on the ability to identify the source of each radio waveform, and to use the time and rate of those emissions to snoop on the persons inside.

The results bordered on the lurid. Now the team at UVA knew when the bathroom was occupied. They pushed further. They knew whether someone was grooming, or showering, or using the toilet. With enough data, they were able to drill down into hidden routines, for example, detecting when food was being prepared, and whether it was a hot or cold meal. The data sketched out lives in rough detail, but they excelled at betraying the patterns of daily life. And humans, as has been noted for millennia, are creatures of fierce habit. Knowing what a person did *today* offers the ability for an eavesdropper to predict, with staggering accuracy, what that person will do *tomorrow*.

There were gaps in these reconstructions, and one important catch—although the homes were all real, they had been fitted with a suite of wireless sensors and controllers. The goal of the study was less about exposing a current danger than analyzing threats and vulnerabilities to come. And they will be coming: Specifically, the team was concerned with the increasing popularity of wireless devices in the home, from the motion sensors that turn lights on and off, to the wireless controllers that allow for home automation—dimming the lights and piping music into specific rooms with a single button push, or cranking on every light when a security alarm is triggered—without a major rewiring job. Some 5 million homes already have similar systems, and the latest estimates suggest that by 2016, 12 million new systems will ship every year. The researchers used off-the-shelf devices from the category's biggest manufacturer, X10, for their test, creating a simulation of tomorrow's status quo. There, so-called smart homes will offer total, centralized control of lighting, heating, and security, for improved energy efficiency, and the gadgety thrill of orchestrating the functions of an entire house (or larger, shared residence, like a nursing home or dorm) from a single computer. "Millions of homes are already vulnerable to the FATS attack, and new systems are being deployed at an ever increasing rate," the team at Virginia argues.

The researchers also pointed out that, while their own gear was relatively complex—the average stalker or burglar isn't sporting a high-frequency oscilloscope and custom-coded algorithms to analyze a week or more of collected transmissions—technology inevitably becomes more accessible, and more intuitive. Legitimate uses for network finger-printing will supply the hardware and software that can be modified or subverted for illegitimate purposes. While a widespread assault on home automation systems has yet to materialize, the researchers claim that current attacks are technically possible, and that "snooping on these devices is as easy as driving around with an X10 receiver to receive unencrypted X10 camera data."

> LEGITIMATE USES FOR NETWORK FINGER-PRINTING WILL SUPPLY THE HARDWARE AND SOFTWARE THAT CAN BE MODIFIED OR SUBVERTED FOR ILLEGITIMATE PURPOSES.

The implication isn't that vans full of hackers are prowling small-town communities, hungrily watching their laptop screens for a signal lock. The point is that, with determination, interior lives can be laid bare. And the more high-tech the home, the more easily it can be cased. And that's just the beginning.

HACKING THE HOME

At a computer security event in 2009—the ominously-named Black Hat USA conference in Las Vegas, a reference to the "bad guy" side of the security spectrum—Mike Davis, a researcher from the consulting firm IOActive presented a simulated attack on smart meters that could theoretically cut power to entire neighborhoods. By Davis' calculations, a computer worm could exploit inherent network weaknesses and surge through a region, infecting some 15,000 meters in 24 hours. The same functions that allow a utility to reduce electricity supply to a home, in order to save the entire grid from a blackout, could give the worm's author veto power over every compromised meter. "Of course we haven't tested it, because nobody in their right mind is going to let us try something in the real world," Davis said during a follow-up presentation about the simulated worm. However the IOActive team did conduct real, over-the-air hacks of real meters, which were either bought on eBay, or dug out of the dumpsters behind utility companies.

In 2010, the security consulting firm InGuardians caused another minor panic with its own smart grid-related presentation, at the Toorcon hacker conference in San Diego. Hoping to shore up potential security gaps among its utility and infrastructure-based clients, the InGuardians' report highlighted the potential for devastating hacks of a simple smart home setup. Just as WiFi connections can act as a gateway for savvy, local intruders to gain access to a computer or network, a reasonably skilled hacker could insinuate himself into other wireless connections. For example, a smart thermostat that uses Zigbee—a low-power wireless protocol that's similar to WiFi, but used almost exclusively to network appliances, medical equipment, and other electronics—to control a home's heating and cooling systems could be hijacked remotely. A relatively simple (by hacker standards) DIY transmitter would allow someone to launch the attack while parked nearby the home. Once the network was compromised, the intruder could easily set the system to repeat a specific command or function over and over, in an infinite loop. A routine message, to open a water control valve by one degree, could repeat until the valve is jammed open.

> ONCE THE NETWORK WAS COMPROMISED, THE INTRUDER COULD EASILY SET THE SYSTEM TO REPEAT A SPECIFIC COMMAND OR FUNCTION OVER AND OVER, IN AN INFINITE LOOP.

In plain terms, these security firms are forecasting the dawn of the house-jack—the capacity to cripple or destroy a home's heating and water systems, to cut off its supply off electricity, or plunge whole streets and neighborhoods into darkness. It might not be immediately clear why someone would want to do those things—but researchers fear the answer might be as simple as "because they can." "Where these vulnerabilities may have gone unnoticed before, when you add the ability to disconnect someone's home, remotely, from electricity, you sort of create this high value on that target," IOActive's Davis says. "Somebody will eventually compromise that target."

What all of these rehearsed and simulated attacks have in common is data—the decrypting and the commandeering of radio transmissions flowing into, from, and throughout the home. But data is only as safe as the devices it travels between—the millions of networked computers that now fill American homes, embedded discreetly in products that don't seem to belong in the same conversation as hackers, viruses and worms. In the rush to add wireless connectivity to every conceivable product, from fridges and toasters to flat-panel TVs, device-makers have invited the black hats right into the house.

THIEVES IN THE TV

The quasi-poetic term is the "Internet of things." It means that the objects that populate our homes are attaching to existing wireless networks, or pairing with one another via Zigbee, Bluetooth, or a host of other protocols, creating new networks. For the most part, the connected machines are talking amongst themselves. An alarm clock tells the coffee maker to start brewing. An electric car informs a smartphone that it's done charging. And every so often, a smart meter receives a blackout warning, and demands fewer cycles from the refrigerator's compressor, and gives the air conditioner a half-hour break.

Much like the regular Internet, the thing-based internet is growing rapidly. Today, embedded computers outnumber PCs five to one. By 2015, analysts predict anywhere from 20 billion to a trillion such internet-connected devices will exist. "We are entering the third wave of computing," says Adrian Turner, CEO of Mocana, a security firm that specializes in embedded devices. "The first was mainframe-centric. The second was PC-centric. The third is device-centric. And it's huge. It's an order of magnitude bigger in terms of the amount of knowledge connecting to networks."

To the average person, knowing that his or her possessions are trading bursts of machine-code is little more than geeky trivia. These newly chattering objects are locked in a private, but impossibly boring conversation, about topics as scintillating as the current temperature in various rooms, and in wordless dialects that aren't worth deciphering. Most embedded devices are designed to fade into the background, to look and perform like smarter versions of classic gadgets. The LCD screen on the refrigerator door doesn't sound a Windows or Mac chime before displaying the weather forecast.

THE LCD SCREEN ON THE REFRIGERATOR DOOR DOESN'T SOUND A WINDOWS OR MAC CHIME BEFORE DISPLAYING THE WEATHER FORECAST.

For those with a moderate knowledge of wireless network protocols, however, these devices no longer speak in tongues. Their commands are clear. They can be intercepted or duplicated. And for hackers of any real skill, these networks could hardly be easier targets. While PCs have developed a sprawling ecosystem of security products and services, embedded devices are largely on their own. Even if an equivalent of Norton or McAfee software existed for these products, most customers would have no way of accessing their refrigerator's operating system (OS), much less installing a new application.

The black hats have no such access issues. The University of Virginia snooping test, as well as the smart grid hacks, proved that dedicated attackers can access a device's network by simply getting close enough. In many cases, though, there's a more traditional way in. The internet of things includes devices attached to the larger internet. They're just dangling there, waiting to be preyed upon.

According to many computer security experts, it's only a matter of time before the internet of things faces a full-scale invasion. The specific risks and attack vectors are as diverse as the connected things themselves, but in 2010, Mocana highlighted one of the most vulnerable classes of targets: Internet-connected TVs.

Millions of flat-panels are already able to join a local wireless network, most often to stream videos from services such as Netflix or YouTube. Every major HDTV maker is now rolling out models with network capability, and it's estimated that by 2014, annual shipments of internet-connected TVs will reach 118 million.

By sending one of these TVs a malicious computer script—not through a direct connection, or by planting it deep within the hardware's operating system, but by slipping the code into the standard datastream—Mocana researchers took control of the device's internet functions. They could insert bogus screens, asking for the user to fill out bank account or credit card information. With the injection of an additional script, they could siphon away the information that had already been used to access Netflix, Twitter, or other password-protected services. The user's browsing privacy was also compromised. The script could collect and report exactly what sites were visited, and when.

WITH THE INJECTION OF AN ADDITIONAL SCRIPT, THEY COULD SIPHON AWAY THE INFORMATION THAT HAD ALREADY BEEN USED TO ACCESS NETFLIX, TWITTER, OR OTHER PASSWORD-PROTECTED SERVICES.

If Mocana's attack had been real, it would have gone unchallenged by the TV's own operating system (which had no way of verifying incoming scripts, or scanning for malicious installations), and unnoticed by individual customers. This was, in fact, a concern when Sony admitted in April 2011 that its database of 77 million PlayStation Network users had been hacked a week earlier. Identity theft was the obvious immediate threat—but at least customers would likely soon know if someone was fraudulently using their credit card number. But what if millions of Internet-connected PlayStation 3 (PS3) owners were tricked into installing some malicious firmware update? What could hackers do with that zombie network—without the gamers ever even knowing?

Although Mocana's CEO claims that manufacturers are attempting to deal with these and other vulnerabilities, the challenge of safeguarding every species of smart device is daunting. "We were fortunate with PCs that Wintel dominated the industry," said Turner, referring to the Windows software and Intel-built CPU chips that are found in most desktops and laptops. "Security was able to coalesce around a single platform. Today, with embedded devices, we have 2458 combinations of OS and CPU that we have to deal with."

For now, we have to take the device makers at their word, that they are prioritizing security with their new product lines. It's a race against the clock, though, with no clear, systemic solutions, and few assurances that PC-like safeguards will ever truly protect tomorrow's smart homes, and the smart devices that fill them.

It's possible that all of these scenarios—stalking via radio waves, houses hijacked out of sheer malice, or TVs that steal your credit card numbers—might seem a little too villainous, too intentional to be a widespread threat. The real danger could be something far sloppier, and far more disturbing.

In early 2005, for instance, hundreds of thousands of computers across the United States were attacked by a "botnet." At the time, it was a cutting edge scam—a trio of hackers (including two minors) had coded a virus that was unwittingly downloaded by users surfing the Internet. The virus turned those computers into a robotic network of zombie PCs, which then attacked other computers networked with the infected host. The botnet installed a sleazy bundle of code, called adware, that forced infected computers to display advertisements. The hackers received a small commission—which ultimately amounted to $100,000—every time the ads popped up. But those ads weren't merely a nuisance: They came at such a rapid-fire clip—even if the computer was no longer connected to the Internet—they often froze PCs, crippled email accounts, and crashed networks.

THE VIRUS TURNED THOSE COMPUTERS INTO A ROBOTIC NETWORK OF ZOMBIE PCS, WHICH THEN ATTACKED OTHER COMPUTERS NETWORKED WITH THE INFECTED HOST.

Twenty-year-old Christopher Maxwell and his partners first compromised computers at California State University-Northridge, UCLA and the University of Michigan—but as the virus leapt from one computer to the next, the hackers had no control over where it would end up. Completely disabling the computer labs across California's Colton Unified School District, for instance, hadn't been Maxwell's specific goal. Neither had been infecting Defense Department computers at more than 400 locations around the world—which quickly made the young men enemies of some very influential people. But the clearest and most present danger—frighteningly illustrating computers' control today over the places we live and work—emerged when the virus struck Seattle's Northwest Hospital and Medical Center. As computers in the intensive care unit succumbed to the virus, they in turn became part of the attack, flooding the system with malicious code. Roughly 150 machines were taken over before the hospital's network buckled under the force of the infection.

Doctors' pagers ceased to work. So did their magnetic keycards, locking doors to operating rooms in front of them. The hospital's advanced diagnostic imaging and laboratory information systems got hit. Nurses scrambled to deliver files, running through the hallways when the electronic file-sharing system melted down; others were recruited as de facto security guards, studying nametags and badges outside checkpoints. Suddenly that simple scheme to install popup ads on a few computers legitimately threatened peoples' lives.

To the hospital staff's credit, they weathered the three-day electronic storm without sacrificing patient care. Furthermore, they alerted the FBI immediately, allowing investigators to collect evidence in the midst of the attack and jumpstart their case. Soon, Maxwell and his fellow conspirators were apprehended.

The true danger of the attack was made clear by the U.S. Attorney's Office, though Maxwell's ultimate sentence—a three-year prison term, along with restitution of $114,000 to Northwest Hospital and $138,000 to the Department of Defense—was significantly less than the government sought. After all, the botnet wasn't designed to turn off physical devices or partially shut down a hospital. That was just collateral damage to a get-rich-quick scheme.

In the years since, botnets have become a global security crisis, with active infections of millions of computers. They're spreading right now, still targeting PCs, oblivious to the smart meters and wireless controllers and embedded devices surrounding them. That's the funny thing about bots. Even if they could predict the collateral damage they're capable of inflicting, they couldn't possibly care less.

CHAPTER 4

WHO'S SPYING ON YOUR PHONE

AT A HACKER CONFERENCE IN JULY 2010, security researcher Chris Paget warned everyone in the room to avoid making any calls. Specifically, those with AT&T cell phones. "As far as your cell phones are concerned, I am now indistinguishable from AT&T," he told the crowd gathered in a meeting room at the Riviera Hotel & Casino in Las Vegas. Paget's $1500 home-built contraption had already tricked some 30 handsets in the room into connecting to it. Any call made from those phones, including encrypted ones, would now route through the mock cell tower, and record onto an attached USB thumb drive. Paget had kept his demonstration intentionally narrow— with more money, and less regard for the FCC, he could spoof other cellular networks, and cover more airspace. In fact, he claimed that if he hooked the system up to the amplifier and jammer he had brought with him, the magnified signal might "knock out all Las Vegas call systems."

In early 2011, at the Black Hat security conference in Arlington, Virginia, a pair of cybersecurity researchers from Spain took the hack to the next, inevitable level. Using a $10,000 set up, they were able to completely intercept the data streams from local smartphones. Calls could be snooped, web sites replaced with imposters, and passwords hijacked. The Spanish team wasn't willing to demo the system live (the FCC was still hounding Paget for his own stunt), but showed a video of a user's bank password being compromised by a phishing site, beamed to the phone's browser from the fake base station.

Then, in March 2011, came another form of phone-jacking. Google pulled 21 applications out of its Android Marketplace, where owners of smartphones running on the Android operating system can download various programs, many of them for free. The targeted apps were loaded with malware. Some were merely nuisances. One piece of malware, however, stunned the security world. "It was able to gain full access to the phone. Full privileges," says Roel Schouwenberg, Senior Malware Researcher at Kaspersky Lab, which specializes in antivirus products. The intrusion wasn't limited to the phone's browser or applications. The malware could theoretically take control of every core function of the device, placing calls as well as eavesdropping on them. The irony is that the security software developed by companies like Kaspersky for Android has nowhere near that level of access. So this type of malware is able to nest deep within the operating system, untouchable to the apps designed to find and eliminate it. "It's the first

THE MALWARE COULD THEORETICALLY TAKE CONTROL OF EVERY CORE FUNCTION OF THE DEVICE, PLACING CALLS AS WELL AS EAVESDROPPING ON THEM.

very serious case, where we're effectively being out-tricked. The malware doesn't have to play by the rules. It grabs control of the entire device, while we're stuck in a box."

These are echoes of what's to come, if cellular providers, phonemakers, and the developers of smartphone operating systems don't retool their products. They're also a frightening nod to what's quietly going on today: In December 2011, once the Android-iPhone geolocation imbroglio died down, 25-year-old Trevor Eckhart discovered that software on his Android-powered phone called Carrier IQ wasn't just logging the location of the device, but also everything he did with it—including when calls were placed, the keys he pressed, contents of text messages, and the websites he visited.

The company's eponymous software is a "diagnostic tool," Carrier IQ says, used to "improve the quality of the network, understand device issues, and ultimately improve the user experience." Roughly 140 million devices worldwide already have it running behind the scenes, sending information back to carriers about how customers use their phones. Sprint, T-Mobile, and AT&T were using the software ostensibly to monitor performance on their networks, in HTC, Motorola, LG, Samsung, and BlackBerry handsets, among others. Soon, iPhone customers discovered Carrier IQ embedded in Apple's mobile operating system, as well.

Eckhart was uncomfortable with the amount of data being surreptitiously gathered. He set up a website, androidsecuritytest.com, to chronicle his findings—complete with selections from the company's own training manuals describing the software's functionality. He labeled Carrier IQ a "rootkit," meaning malicious software that has privileged access to a device while hiding its presence. Clearly ruffled, Carrier IQ fired off a cease-and-desist letter, threatening Eckhart with $150,000 in damages for publishing those copyrighted training materials—before ultimately withdrawing the letter and apologizing when the Electronic Frontier Foundation stepped in to support the researcher.

Carrier IQ maintains that the data gathered about users is hardly the stuff of Hollywood plot lines. But there's no mistaking its creepiness. According to the company's own advertisement of its Mobile Service Intelligence Platform (MSIP) and IQ Insight offerings, "We know you don't just want data, you want to solve business problems and identify new business opportunities... What's more, the combination of the MSIP and IQ Insight lets you move seamlessly from broad trend data across many users, through comparative groups down to diagnostic data from individual devices. Now, not only can you identify trends, you have the power to drill down to specific instances, giving you the insight your specialists need to make a difference."

For the moment, evidence of actual damages from phone hacks is practically non-existent. (The biggest example of real harm has come from China, where over a million cellphones were taken over in 2011, and made to pump out text message spam. Customers' bills exploded, at least temporarily.) Carrier IQ's software, however, touched on the most visceral fear when it comes to telephone privacy, that a silent third party in the background could be listening, recording, compiling.

CARRIER IQ'S SOFTWARE, HOWEVER, TOUCHED ON THE MOST VISCERAL FEAR WHEN IT COMES TO TELEPHONE PRIVACY, THAT A SILENT THIRD PARTY IN THE BACKGROUND COULD BE LISTENING, RECORDING, COMPILING.

Unfortunately, your carrier's diagnostic tools may be the least of your worries—because the chances the government is packing away some fragment of your phone data, if not entire calls? Are surprisingly good. While stalking the telecommunication networks for the public enemies of various eras, the state has stumbled onto a Rosetta Stone of privacy threats, with the potential to automate nearly every form of mass-intrusion. All thanks to a few bootleggers and suicide bombers.

BRANDEIS AND THE BOOTLEGGER

It should have been a moment of triumph, decades in the making. In 1928, eight years into Prohibition, known bootlegger and ex-police officer Roy Olmstead was charging the government with illegally wiretapping his phones. Like a sleeper agent suddenly activated after a lifetime in hiding, Louis Brandeis found himself a justice in the United States Supreme Court, presiding over its first case of alleged illegal wiretapping.

This was the same Brandeis who, 38 years earlier, had co-written the landmark legal article, "The Right to Privacy," a darkly prescient warning of technology's ability to penetrate our lives. Since then, Brandeis had risen to the highest court in the land, and had contributed to pivotal decisions, but never one so close to the cause that had helped vault him into the spotlight of his profession.

The facts of the case were simple. At the core of Olmstead v. the United States was a possible breach of the Fourth Amendment—federal agents from the Bureau of Investigation (forerunner to the FBI) had tapped the phones of Seattle, Washington's biggest bootlegger. No warrants were requested. Olmstead argued that this amounted to an illegal search and seizure. He was so positive, in fact, that he claimed to have known about the taps for years, after a dirty agent supposedly offered to sell him the growing piles of transcripts. Olmstead balked, continued using at least six phone lines to take orders, and made sure to pepper his conversations with personal digs at the BOI team's lead investigator. He had faith in the Constitution's narrow but unerring defense of privacy, and in the fact that state laws found such taps inadmissible.

As ad hoc Constitutional scholars go, Olmstead wasn't alone. Most states restricted such techniques, or threw them out of court outright. Mabel Walker Willebrandt, the attorney who specialized in arguing Prohibition cases before the Supreme Court, was so opposed to wire-tapping evidence, she refused to participate. It was precisely the kind of threat Brandeis had predicted. This, finally, was his chance to take a stand, and bolster the borders of private life against yet another invasion. When the court handed down its ruling, the bench was divided: four votes to three, against Olmstead.

The conviction was upheld, and the associated warrantless wire-tapping was approved. Writing the majority opinion, Chief Justice and former United States President William Taft conjured that familiar refrain in privacy skirmishes—the reasonable expectation of privacy, and, here, the lack of it. Because the taps were installed in public, intercepted on lines outside Olmstead's property, there was no invasion, lawful or otherwise. As for the calls themselves, in an era when any phone connection could be listened in on by a nosy switchboard operator, there was nothing to search, nothing to seize. A call was no more sacrosanct than an in-person conversation. That the gathered exchanges filled 700 pages of transcripts used as evidence against Olmstead was beside the point—the Fourth Amendment did not apply.

SINCE THE TAPS WERE INSTALLED IN PUBLIC, INTERCEPTED ON LINES OUTSIDE OLMSTEAD'S PROPERTY, THERE WAS NO INVASION, LAWFUL OR OTHERWISE.

Brandeis was left to write the longest of the dissenting opinions. It would become his legacy. "Subtler and more far-reaching means of invading privacy have become available to the Government," he wrote. "Discovery and invention have made it possible for the Government, by means far more effective than stretching upon the rack, to obtain disclosure in court of what is whispered in the closet."

That last phrase is lifted almost verbatim from his old journal article, when Brandeis and Warren could only guess that, some day, "what is whispered in the closet shall be proclaimed from the house-tops.' " At issue now was more than the capture of your face by way of Kodak, and the dissemination of your life in print, because of curiosity or profit, Here, the government was siphoning off your communication, neatly filing the tawdry details next to the mundane ones, the relevant aside the merely intimate.

Brandeis tried to summon the Constitution's framers to his side, or at least guess at their intentions toward privacy. "They knew that only a part of the pain, pleasure and satisfactions of life are to be found in material things. They sought to protect Americans in their beliefs, their thoughts, their emotions and their sensations. They conferred, as against the Government, the right to be let alone—the most comprehensive of rights, and the right most valued by civilized men."

Though he still considered technology the prime catalyst in eroding privacy, Brandeis also pointed out the most powerful social driver in these intrusions. Not a sophisticated, malicious campaign of Big Brotherhood, but a more accidental, gradual shuffle towards the exposure of all secrets, at the whim of heroes. "The greatest dangers to liberty lurk in insidious encroachment by men of zeal," he wrote, "well meaning but without understanding."

Nowhere did Brandeis lay the blame for the wiretaps at the feet of Prohibition. But in the aftermath of the court's verdict, the Olmstead case helped shatter any residual faith in the Noble Experiment. Much of the public was outraged, and after serving his four-year sentence, Olmstead received a full presidential pardon, and a reversal of his fine, in 1935. Prohibition was itself repealed in 1933. Brandeis's dissent would be referenced in countless cases to come, and was considered integral to subsequent federal regulations on wiretaps, as well as another Supreme

Court case in 1967, which ruled the warrantless taps of payphones inadmissible. History, and the majority of Americans, would agree with his rejection of unchecked surveillance. In defeat, Brandeis may have managed something like a victory, after all.

SPYING GOES DOMESTIC

The Olmstead case was a watershed moment for privacy advocates. It solidified a growing national disquiet towards the measures taken by "men of zeal" on our behalf. It exposed what was possible, without permission, based on the assumptions of a few. In particular, it turned warrantless wiretapping into a criminal act.

But as we've already seen, threats to privacy never die. They adapt, and recur. In December 2005 the *New York Times* broke the story on a sweeping government program to spy on the phone calls of American citizens throughout the country. Warrantless wiretaps had returned, on a scale that dwarfed anything deployed against Olmstead and other bootleggers. The desperate times of Prohibition had been supplanted by the existential terror of 9/11. The response, naturally, was enhanced.

ARMED WITH AN EXECUTIVE ORDER SIGNED BY THE PRESIDENT IN 2002, THE COURTS WERE BYPASSED COMPLETELY.

Though the full details of the wiretapping program may never be disclosed, when the *Times* article was released, it was believed to be limited to international calls, where at least one party had suspected connections to terrorists. Normally, this would require a visit to the Federal Intelligence Services Court and a warrant. Armed with an executive order signed by the president in 2002, the courts were bypassed completely.

Like the Olmstead verdict, the warrantless wiretapping program drew outrage. It was labeled domestic spying by critics, and remains the Platonic ideal of mass surveillance gone amok. Then-President George W. Bush was the target of much of the furor—his Justice Department suffered the rest. Later, reports surfaced that the plan had been pushed through without Attorney General John Ashcroft's support; the attorney general had been visited while hospitalized after gall bladder surgery, and even in his heavily medicated state Ashcroft mustered enough strength to reject it.

This was a conspiracy theorist's nightmare come true, a project so secret it had no official name—nothing so evocative as other mass surveillance projects, such as Echelon, Carnivore, and Total Information Awareness. It was the bastard lovechild of a small cadre of politicians, and the always nebulous National Security Agency.

Of course, all of this has been rehashed in the national media. But in the years following the *Times*' initial story, as each new revelation made global headlines, a new reality set in. Anonymous sources reported that the restriction to international communications was bogus—domestic calls had been tapped, as well. Testifying before Congress, Attorney General Alberto Gonzales (Ashcroft's successor) admitted that the surveillance had begun almost immediately after 9/11, when Congress granted Bush the right to use force against Al Qaeda, months before the president's 2002 executive order. The *Times* and other outlets uncovered evidence that additional NSA programs were collecting data on domestic calls, without actually recording content. In 2007, major U.S. phone carriers admitted to granting unprecedented access to intelligence agencies, to assist in their surveillance and data gathering. And in 2009, ex-NSA analyst Russell Tice, who had served as the initial whistleblower for the *Times* story, told MSNBC's Keith Olbermann that the NSA had conducted mass analysis of American citizens' phone calls, using software to identify potential targets.

"This is garnered from algorithms that have been put together to try to just dream-up scenarios that might be information that is associated with how a terrorist could operate," Tice told Olbermann. "And once that information gets to the NSA ... they start looking for word-recognition, if someone just talked about the daily news and mentioned something about the Middle East they could easily be brought to the forefront of having that little flag put by their name that says 'potential terrorist.'"

IN 2007, MAJOR U.S. PHONE CARRIERS ADMITTED TO GRANTING UNPRECEDENTED ACCESS TO INTELLIGENCE AGENCIES, TO ASSIST IN THEIR SURVEILLANCE AND DATA GATHERING.

Since he first went public as the *Times*' primary source, the larger picture painted by Tice has been of an agency eavesdropping on an entire populace, tying recorded phone calls to credit card records and other personal data, creating vast databases of individuals with no confirmed links to terrorism.

It's possible that Tice is exaggerating. After all, he was released from the NSA in relative disgrace, before he began leaking information to the *New York Times*. But between the broad strokes of his story, with its millions of victims and untold terabytes of stored phone calls and profiles, Tice is describing a risk that transcends even the post-9/11 phone surveillance initiative, in all its sprawling menace. A billion recorded phone calls is disturbing, but imagine managing that ocean of data, devoting an entire career to indexing the conversations of a country, on the off chance that a handful will be damning.

No, the danger is in the software that chews through unspeakable amounts of information, in all its digitized forms, and reorganizes the known world, weaving our daily activities, our verifiable past, and our suspected future into branched connections.

In the hunt for those connections, mistakes will be made. And privacy, if it can survive the code, becomes irrelevant.

NON-OBVIOUS RELATIONSHIPS

The algorithms that Tice was referring to, that "dream-up scenarios" of terrorist activity, can be traced back to the most surveilled places on Earth: casinos. Originating in the Mirage in Las Vegas, as a way to identify potential cheaters on the premises, this type of software searches for "non-obvious relationships," or NORs. "We created the software for the gaming industry," Jeff Jonas, founder of Systems Research & Development, told *Popular Mechanics* in 2010. "Now it's used as business intelligence for banks, insurance companies and retailers."

Those are the deployments Jonas openly supports, where the parameters are reasonably defined, and the goal is to boost profits through analysis—the injection of his NORA, or non-obvious relationship awareness, software into the playbook of large-scale electronic surveillance is more contentious. Jonas travelled to the headquarters of DARPA, the Pentagon's advanced research division, after the 9/11 attacks, and was involved for years with attempts to integrate NORA in the Total Information Awareness program. But by 2005, Jonas' doubts about NORA's effectiveness at detecting terrorists were well-known.

NORA gathers disparate data and extracts patterns. In a Vegas casino, NORA can sniff out connections between dealers and suspicious players—whether they had lived together at some point, stayed in the same hotel room, or otherwise crossed paths before meeting at the game table.

Searching for patterns of terrorist activity is a very different task. Calling a suspected terrorist might be considered an obvious relationship. Making frequent calls to Pakistan, whether to your relatives, or a business associate, and to no one who is red-flagged by various federal agencies or found on any watch list, is less obvious. But if that non-watch-listed, non-flagged individual happens to also keep in touch with rogue elements in Pakistan, your phone calls could be considered a NOR to various extremist groups operating in the Middle East.

This use of NORA requires data to produce results, and more data to validate those results, and to generate new, ever-larger patterns. Additional datapoints, from basic call data to keyword-filtered recordings of those conversations, are all grist for the mill.

This could be considered a criticism of any deployment of NORA, that it can always benefit from information, and that any conclusion it draws is a work in progress. But where the private sector must limit itself to publicly available data, the government can dig deeper. To make NORA or any related software useful, warrants must sidestepped. No court could keep up with the pace of data collection. The ends justify the means, and the means demand endlessly more data.

PRIVACY INTRUSIONS AND THE NEW FACTS OF LIFE

Officially, NORA's continued existence within the NSA's surveillance programs is a matter of debate. The Total Information Awareness program, which took the lead in testing the software's terrorist-hunting functionality, lost its funding in 2003. The former deputy of TIA has since claimed that the software transitioned to the NSA, along with other elements of the program. NORA is also central to the arguments made by critics like Tice, that while gathering fodder for NOR pattern-matching, intelligence agencies inevitably collected vast swaths of information about the random and innocent, bystanders in a data-fueled hunt for terrorists. To date, the government has yet to publicly recognize a single related arrest. If Tice and others are even half-right, Americans have been spied on wholesale, with no benefits worth celebrating.

Maybe NORA is dead. Maybe the trolling of millions of phone logs for that single whiff of blood spilled, or fresh carnage ahead, is over. There's no reason to think so. A steady stream of attempts to end the warrantless wiretapping program, and the entire campaign of warrantless surveillance that its exposure revealed, have all failed. Decisions handed down by state and federal judges go nowhere, and investigations by groups like the ACLU and Electronic Frontier Foundation do little to produce tangible change. A public records request by the ACLU in August 2011, for instance, revealed that hundreds of local police departments throughout the country anonymously track cell phone locations, often without a warrant, and with virtually zero court oversight. "The practice is so common that cell phone companies have manuals for police explaining what data the companies store, how much they charge police to access that data, and what officers need to do to get it," the ACLU wrote in its report. But few expect practices like that to actually change.

THE TOTAL INFORMATION AWARENESS PROGRAM, WHICH TOOK THE LEAD IN TESTING THE SOFTWARE'S TERRORIST HUNTING FUNCTIONALITY, LOST ITS FUNDING IN 2003.

"A lot of privacy advocacy has this quality of the drunk guy looking for his keys where the light is best," says Jim Harper, Director of Information Policy Studies at the Cato Institute. "We talk about identity theft and Facebook, and we can grasp what to do there. But we have no way to bust the federal government for wiretapping our communications. They bottled up the court system to protect the Bush administration. We know from leaks that these privacy invasions were astounding. But we just have to take it, because it's so hard to stop."

Wiretapping remains a fact of life in the United States. It's occurring with a frequency and sophistication we can only glimpse, and never confirm. And by a route no one, even Brandeis, could have predicted, its helped incubate a pattern-matching

WIRETAPPING REMAINS A FACT OF LIFE IN THE UNITED STATES.

approach to privacy intrusion that cuts across the private and government sectors, and joins nearly every major industry in a single mode of attack. Eavesdropping, like scanning for faces or tracking someone's current location and daily routines, used to be an inefficient grind, powered by long hours and excessive caffeine. Those were sporadic, isolated events. The rules of the game have changed. The computers are rewriting them, faster than ever.

CHAPTER 5

WHO'S SPYING ON YOUR COMPUTER

MODERN LIFE IS ONLY A PARTLY DIGITAL THING. The places we travel are physical destinations. The paths we choose are navigated by mechanics, forged in steel or flesh and bone. Our secrets aren't binary.

Computers, meanwhile, are simply information brokers. When asked, they consult one another, and report back with search results, satellite maps, product reviews. They are unbiased attendants and witnesses.

For those who care about privacy, computers are also the greatest of all possible traitors. Every topic we've covered revolves around some form of silicon snitching. Faces can be scanned and catalogued, but it takes an algorithm to match one set of cheekbones to a known criminal's. Homes and appliances are impossible to hack from the outside, until they're studded with network-attached computers. And software has sidestepped a century of legal battles over telephone eavesdropping, as powerful code creates target lists, pulls keywords out of conversations, and draws scattered bits of data into profiles of American citizens, archived and reviewed without their knowledge.

If it's a war, then the invaders have won nearly every battle. For each judge who bans the use of warrantless GPS trackers, countless users have their location data extracted and filed away by a smartphone or application maker. The amount of spyware latching onto browsers and burrowing into hard drives is growing, despite near-universal awareness of the risks associated with suspicious websites and email attachments. As we'll see in the following chapters, once-disparate hackers have gathered into anarchic armies, collectively dragging down the servers of Sony, Citibank, and other corporate juggernauts.

THE AMOUNT OF SPYWARE LATCHING ONTO BROWSERS AND BURROWING INTO HARD DRIVES IS GROWING, DESPITE NEAR-UNIVERSAL AWARENESS OF THE RISKS ASSOCIATED WITH SUSPICIOUS WEBSITES AND EMAIL ATTACHMENTS.

It's not yet entirely hopeless. For reasons that aren't completely clear, a showdown has emerged in a specific area of digital privacy: online tracking. It's a struggle over the ability of strangers to know the sites you visit, the things you've bought or considered buying, the places you've gone and plan to still see, and to create detailed profiles that are passed out to a network of buyers.

How this fight ends could mark a turning point for those trying to safeguard privacy. Or, it could be more of the intrusive same.

THE GENIE IS OUT OF THE BOTTLE

On April 1, 2004, Google redefined email. The invite-only, April Fools' Day launch of Gmail couldn't have been more serious for AOL and Yahoo!, the reigning giants of web-based email services. Gmail offered what was effectively unlimited storage space—1 GB, with the promise of more as additional servers came online—for free, an exponential gain over its competitors.

There was a price to be paid, though. Alongside the user's email window appeared a column of text-only advertisements that seemed at times eerily aware of your interests, and at others clumsily presumptuous. An incoming message with dinner plans shared the screen with ads for restaurants. A reference to death in an email triggered offers from funeral homes—or talk of visiting Vancouver, ads for head shops.

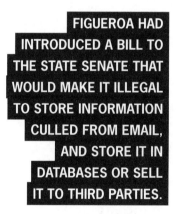

FIGUEROA HAD INTRODUCED A BILL TO THE STATE SENATE THAT WOULD MAKE IT ILLEGAL TO STORE INFORMATION CULLED FROM EMAIL, AND STORE IT IN DATABASES OR SELL IT TO THIRD PARTIES.

The response was immediate, and not what the Mountain View, California-based company expected. Privacy groups demanded to know who was reading those emails. When Google explained that human eyes never scanned that content, that algorithms were matching keywords in the message to related ads, California State Senator Liz Figueroa sent a letter to the company, requesting that it halt all contextual ads. By May, Figueroa had introduced a bill to the state senate that would make it illegal to store information culled from email, and store it in databases or sell it to third parties. "

The bill passed easily, and moved to the state assembly for another vote. In a statement, Google expressed surprise at the general outcry. "When we began the limited test of Gmail, we expected our service would be the subject of intense interest. What we did not anticipate was the reaction from some privacy activists, editorial writers and legislators, many of whom condemned Gmail without first seeing it for themselves."

In fact, months later, after numerous meetings with Google and others, Figueroa dropped the bill entirely. Gmail, after all, does what its authors claimed—it performs a contained, double-blind experiment in digital marketing, displaying specific, targeted ads, without reporting back to the company's servers who was talking about dinner, death, or anything else. A bill restricting the storage of such information, and the creation of profiles for the purpose of additional targeted advertising would be irrelevant to Gmail. Abandoning it was common sense.

It was also a missed opportunity. When her bill had first passed the state senate, Figueroa told the Associated Press that she worried companies would "use our emails to create profiles on us, based on our most personal and intimate thoughts." She also warned that protocols should be put in place early in the rollout of ad-supported email services, since "once the information genie gets out of the bottle, it is impossible to put back."

THE QUESTION OF CONSENT

Figueroa was more right than she knew. As the creep factor of Gmail's ads faded, and contextual ads became ubiquitous, a bizarre new industry began doing precisely what the senator feared, though with a slightly different strategy. Companies that specialized in online marketing used perfectly legal means to extract information about individual users, based solely on browsing habits.

Now, brick-and-mortar stores have for decades done much the same thing: They build profiles of customers who use loyalty program cards, then send coupons to specific clientele. Some stores, like Target, go further with their demographic logging, bolstering those shopping records with things like the customer's age, estimated salary, the credit cards they carry in their wallets, and their marital status. (The depth of information is so revealing that in one high-profile example, Target was able to analyze the shift in purchase patterns for a young woman in Minnesota, and thus mail ads to her home for expectant mothers—even before the teenager had mentioned anything to her parents about a baby.)

The primary difference between the record-keeping done by grocery stores chains and online tracking is consent. Signing up for gas points at Stop & Shop is a known trade-off, relinquishing the right to privacy in exchange for some tangible discount. The average person online, however, doesn't assume his or her every move is being broadcast. After all, the internet isn't available because of a contractual agreement with its advertisers. Most users pay service providers for a monthly connection.

THE PRIMARY DIFFERENCE BETWEEN THE RECORD-KEEPING DONE BY GROCERY STORES CHAINS AND ONLINE TRACKING IS CONSENT.

The rules and restrictions associated with those deals can be arcane, but they don't include surrendering privacy to a network of third parties, automated spies that have turned profiles gathered without your permission into products.

At first, the routine communication between websites and a visitor's computer was basic—such as which browser was being used. Soon, however, the datapoints were tumbling in—the user's language and font settings (a possible indication of ethnicity and age), and the computer's specifications (hinting at affluence, or lack thereof), including the internet protocol (IP) address. The IP address is a particularly powerful numerical sequence. It provides a real-time location for the user, ranging from a given state and town to a specific neighborhood, placing that person within established demographic estimates of political leanings, sexual orientation, as well as creating a kind of bar code for that user, a way to identify them even when names are withheld.

The result is a patchwork of guessed characteristics, possible likes and dislikes, much of which is wrong, but one that is constantly revised and updated as new datapoints are applied to your growing profile. Those profiles are then sold either bundled within databases, or individually. Top-tier tracking firm Blue Kai, for example, auctions off profiles as the smallest of micro-transactions. If a given user books a flight online, that information—the foreknowledge of where that person plans to be, and, therefore, which new hotels, stores, or restaurants they might soon be in contact with—might trade for less than a cent.

Earning profits from such infinitesimally small transactions would be impossible without algorithms. They coordinate the reports flooding in from across the entire internet, attach new data to existing profiles, reconcile conflicts with existing data on those subjects, and, finally, manage the shadow market of profile resale. They also reshape the web around you, sometimes in less-than-desirable ways. A history of buying plane tickets without extensive research into cheaper alternatives could label you as a big spender. That could mean higher ticket prices from future searches, and less discounts in other categories. Because of the hundreds of millions of computers surrendering and coordinating this information without question, and the software that automatically scans that tidal flow of betrayals for value, a practice that barely existed a decade ago is now a multi-billion dollar business.

EARNING PROFITS FROM SUCH INFINITESIMALLY SMALL TRANSACTIONS WOULD BE IMPOSSIBLE WITHOUT ALGORITHMS.

For reference sake, this is a breakdown of the number of companies actively tracking visitors to popular websites, on a single day in 2011, as detected by the online privacy group PrivacyChoice.

Readers of the NewYorkTimes.com were tracked by seven different organizations. TechCrunch, a technology blog that routinely covers online tracking, was watched by 13 trackers. Those numbers, it turned out, were on the low end of the spectrum. Although 21 tracking companies were perched on SuperPages.com, and 33 on gossip blog Perez-Hilton.com, the most-tracked sites included the populist NewYork-Post.com (36) and the San Francisco Chronicle's online portal, SFgate.com (53).

A paranoid person might consider this an ambush—browse the very news sites and blogs that might feature stories about online tracking, and become the latest victim. The truth is less dramatic, and more daunting. The trackers have no reason to target specific sites or users. Being online and being tracked are now one and the same.

"DO NOT TRACK"

In 2009, a study released by researchers from Worcester Polytechnic Institute in Massachusetts and AT&T Labs revealed just how pervasive online tracking had become. The team found that eleven of the twelve largest social networking sites had leaked user information to third parties. Name, gender, age, zip code and more were siphoned off with minimal effort. "If you had a Facebook profile, and you loaded a page with an ad, when your browser pulled that data, part of the data sent to a third-party server was your user ID," says Lee Tien of the Electronic Frontier Foundation, one of the first organizations to draw attention to the study. In one instance, the researchers found that leaked data included users' email addresses, information that wasn't even publicly available to other members of the site. "Now advertisers and marketers could attach the information from your profile to whatever profile they were already building. And they had your IP address, too," says Tien. Where a string of numbers might have once represented a hazy approximation of someone's life based on browsing habits—Hispanic, affluent, mid-forties, married but also scanning dating sites—a social networking profile could fill in the gaps, putting a face, name, friends and family to the digits. The name might never resurface in the open, but the IP address will. So with each future online session, our (fictional) subject's profile is less of an estimate than a running account of his life—one more complete than the version known to those friends and family.

For most of the profiled, the only visible sign of intrusion comes through behavioral advertising. Once enough data has been compiled, those surreptitious visits to dating sites will begin to attract ads for other dating services, which might appear on completely unrelated websites. Another kind of user, researching her newly diagnosed diabetes, starts seeing increasingly more ads for testing kits and mail order insulin. Unlike Gmail's contextual ads,

FOR MOST OF THE PROFILED, THE ONLY VISIBLE SIGN OF INTRUSION COMES THROUGH BEHAVIORAL ADVERTISING.

these customized offers aren't generated through a simple pairing of keywords. They rely on regular, two-way communication with the databases that catalogue our desires—without users ever knowing it, and certainly without their permission.

It's this lack of consent, maybe, coupled with the ubiquitous nature of the internet—the sense that it's another utility, a given, like running water or electricity—that's inspired something new in the history of digital privacy. It's not a letter-writing campaign, or a public scolding of Big Data. It's called Do Not Track, and it has the makings of a true counter-attack.

To understand Do Not Track, it's important to understand browser cookies. First invented in 1994 for e-commerce, these tiny snips of data were originally intended to be helpful. Web navigation is a string of rapid-fire requests and responses—a browser asks to see a page, and each request must be vetted, approved and processed before anything displays on-screen. Cookies create familiarities between browsers and sites, and shortcuts. They typically save to a computer's hard drive on the user's first visit to a site or a specific page, and can do anything from saving the contents of a shopping cart during a single session to keeping a user permanently logged in during return visits.

TRACKING COOKIES ARE THE BACKBONE OF ONLINE ADVERTISING.

Within the larger genus of cookies is a peculiar subspecies. It doesn't load pages faster, or keep you logged-in, or assist your experience in any way. The tracking cookie marks you. Like an ear tag clipped to an endangered animal, it provides a unique identifier, helping advertisers record your visits to sites designed to detect those cookies. It makes you a target.

Tracking cookies are the backbone of online advertising. They enable the creation of user profiles, and the constant revision of those profiles each time the cookie is rediscovered on various sites. Details are grafted on from other, non-browser-based sources, but the tracking cookie is the target's first and constant companion.

In response to criticism, many online marketers offered opt-out cookies to users, additional cookies that would disable the tracking associated with their own ads. Opt-out cookies were effectively useless—they had to be downloaded individually from the dozens of participating advertisers, and were either flushed out during cookie purges (something privacy-minded users do on a regular basis), or programmed to disappear after six months. Worse still, there were advertisers who didn't bother with opt-out cookies at all.

In 2009, security and privacy researcher Chris Soghoian and lead privacy engineer for Mozilla, Sid Stamm, came up with their own opt-out strategy. The Do Not Track (DNT) Header was an extension for the

Firefox browser that accompanied each request for a webpage with a polite, clear request to not be tracked. It also asked for behavioral ads to be blocked. For the DNT Header to work, advertisers would have to actively look for that code, and prevent their cookies from latching on, and specific ads from loading. The advertisers passed.

The DNT Header was stillborn. But as a concept, Do Not Track was gaining momentum. During a Senate hearing on online privacy in 2010, Federal Trade Commission (FTC) Chairman Jon Leibowitz floated the idea of a Do Not Track list, similar to the Do Not Call registry that restricts telemarketers. Later that year, the DNT Header returned, revamped by Stanford University researchers Jonathan Mayer and Arvind Narayanan to leave the issue of behavioral ads alone, and simply indicate an anti-tracking preference. Like its previous incarnation, the header had no inherent power. Advertisers would have to read that request, and choose to honor it.

In December of 2010, the FTC issued an online privacy report that focused on tracking, throwing its support behind a mechanism like the DNT Header. Part of that report was an open threat—if the marketers did not find a viable solution on their own, or embrace a header or other standard protocol, the government would have to take action. Is his opening remarks to Congress on the release of the report, FTC Chairman Jon Leibowitz said, "Some in industry support what we're doing, but we know that others will claim we're going too far. To those highly paid professional naysayers, I have only one question: What are you for? Because it can't be the status quo on privacy."

THE UNKNOWN IMPACT

Judging by its March 10, 2011 cover story, *Time* magazine, has few qualms with the status quo. The feature, by staff writer Joel Stein, details the startling amount of information gathered about him, by companies he does business with, and many who simply track his activities online. Ultimately, Stein is apathetic. "...oddly, the more I learned about data mining, the less concerned I was. Sure, I was surprised that all these companies are actually keeping permanent files on me. But I don't think they will do anything with them that does me any harm," Stein writes. Between the various inaccuracies in those profiles (one company assumed he was a teenage girl), and the lack of any tangible evidence of abuses, Stein sees the tracking as a novel fact of life, not a broader risk.

"I thought that cover story was crap," says Jonathan Mayer, co-creator of the revised DNT Header. "It conflated the end result—that I'm lumped into an interest segment, and then targeted by ads—with concerns over the tracking that's going on in the first place." To privacy advocates like Mayer, the ads aren't the problem. They're evidence of problems still to come. "If you think this is all harmless, let me ask you a question. Would you hand over your web browsing history to someone you haven't met? Of course not. It reveals your interests, your aspirations, everything you sought information on. It's intensely personal."

As advertising provides even greater revenue potential for web titans such as Google, Amazon, Facebook, Twitter, and more, the amount of data mined will only increase. In January, Google made global headlines—and suffered ubsequent backlash—for revamping its privacy policy, allowing the company to track the activities of users as they move across Google's 70 platforms, from Gmail to Google Docs to the search engine to YouTube and beyond. The move will create a deeper profile for each of its users, allowing for a smoother, more integrated experience, the company says—and for more targeted ads thanks to combined datapoints. "For every unique user who goes into their Google preferences and opts out of targeted advertising," says company project manager Jonathan McPhie, "more than nine look at the ads and will do nothing—or they'll say, 'Hey, I'm actually interested in this.'"

Those who defend or merely shrug off anxieties over online tracking point out that no major court cases have demonstrated physical or financial injuries resulting from these browsing profiles. To Jim Brock, founder of PrivacyChoice, that only makes matter worse. "You never know the impact. You never know whether that application for a credit card was denied because they used your email to get to your social profile. Or you didn't get a job because they got to a social profile in a way you didn't anticipate or didn't understand could happen," Brock says.

"YOU NEVER KNOW WHETHER THAT APPLICATION FOR A CREDIT CARD WAS DENIED BECAUSE THEY USED YOUR EMAIL TO GET TO YOUR SOCIAL PROFILE."

The best-case scenario is that tracking profiles have no immediate, negative value. They drive an industry few people know exists, possibly funneling more cash into advertisers, and therefore into the web sites that might otherwise charge fees for access. If they're wrong about us, all the better.

Meanwhile, that data sits on servers scattered around the world. The email addresses lifted without permission, tied to names and addresses and records of the cities we've flown to, hotels we've slept in, and the topics we've searched for and sites we've visited, it's all there, sunk in digital amber, waiting to be put to work.

CHAPTER 6

WHO'S SPYING ON YOUR MONEY

THE GREATEST HACK IN HISTORY was the one that never happened. In the 1983 movie WarGames, a high school student flexes such muscle over all things computerized, he accidentally barges into the deepest recesses of the Pentagon's experimental defense network. There, he initiates a wargame with a supercomputer, and comes close to starting a nuclear war with the Soviet Union. That was America's introduction to computer intrusion, and the subculture that surrounded it. A character played by a young Matthew Broderick— that's how hackers entered mainstream thought.

In hindsight, hackers were an unworthy bogeyman. They weren't harbingers of a networked apocalypse, or accomplished criminals. Like kids whipping stones through the windows of abandoned buildings, they made mischief. They exploited obscure hardware vulnerabilities to commandeer corporate phone systems, and fill voicemail logs with gibberish. They crank-called organizations large and small, fast-talking passwords out of hapless employees, and called it "social engineering," implying that society itself was yet another target to be hacked. When they weren't rifling telephone company dumpsters or brainstorming new, mock-sinister names for themselves or their groups—the Legion of Doom, a reference to a gang of comic book supervillains, was the era's most well-known collective—they would occasionally live up to their growing legend, by actually penetrating computers and lifting credit card information or classified data. Others turned electronic mayhem into a contagion, unleashing the first software viruses and worms, temporarily crippling huge numbers of computers.

But those were the exceptions. Most hackers were simply peeking behind the curtains of power to prove they could. In 1986, Legion of Doom member Lloyd Blankenship, aka "The Mentor," published a manifesto for the hacker mindset, called "The Conscience of a Hacker." "We make use of a service already existing without paying for what could be dirt-cheap if it wasn't run by profiteering gluttons, and you call us criminals," he writes. "Yes, I am a criminal. My crime is that of curiosity. My crime is that of judging people by what they say and think, not what they look like. My crime is that of outsmarting you, something that you will never forgive me for."

In its meandering, condescending insolence, Blankenship's screed remains a pitch-perfect representation of why so many hackers hack. Because they can. Because they're told not to. Hacking is one part self-expression, another part civil disobedience, and veined with bitterness throughout.

To Congress, hacking was also an unprecedented threat. In response to a handful of high-profile hacks, the Computer Fraud and Abuse Act was passed in 1986, turning nearly any computer intrusion into a criminal act. By 1989, the United States Secret Service began targeting hackers. And in 1990, the agency coordinated with local law enforcement in 14 cities to arrest suspected hackers and confiscate their computers. They called it Operation Sundevil. Though it resulted in few convictions, at a time when the global hacking community numbered in the hundreds, and internet access was restricted to roughly 3 million people worldwide, nearly all of those connections made through an employer, Sundevil seemed like a turning point. Teenage troublemakers were being rounded up by the same agents who might otherwise be chasing down million-dollar counterfeiting rings, or diving in front of a presidential assassin's bullet.

IN 1990, THE UNITED STATES SECRET SERVICE COORDINATED WITH LOCAL LAW ENFORCEMENT IN 14 CITIES TO ARREST SUSPECTED HACKERS AND CONFISCATE THEIR COMPUTERS.

In fact, it was a one-sided escalation. Hackers didn't take up arms, or unleash untold carnage across the rapidly expanding internet. As before, they picked at the edges of big business, often doing little more than securing free access or services for themselves, or defacing the webpages of the richer and more powerful. Through the '90s and most of the 2000s they became part of the internet's larger ecosystem, strengthening the defenses of the networks and home computers they attacked, some even transitioning to jobs in cybersecurity.

The fever dream of WarGames had subsided. Hacking couldn't start World War III. It impacted the bottom lines of major corporations, but so did industrial espionage, and stock fluctuations, and all the vagaries of capitalism's second, digital act. Hackers were vandals, petty thieves, and very, very occasionally spies. Nothing for the average person to be concerned with.

THE GAMERS AND THE SPEAR PHISHERMEN

By 2011, hacking had become everyone's problem.

In April, an unidentified group of hackers brought down Sony's Play-Station Network, a free, online gaming and entertainment service with 77 million customers worldwide. A few days into the outage, Sony revealed just how bad the data breach was. Though no evidence was produced, the company believed it possible that an "unauthorized individual" may have gained access to users' credit card information, along with associated names and physical addresses. Worse, the number of potential victims eventually rose to 100 million.

The network stayed down for close to a month, during which time members (the author included) were locked out, unable to log in and either change or delete sensitive information. The financial blow to Sony, whose PlayStation 3 console already lagged behind Microsoft's competing Xbox 360 game system and network, was significant—estimates ranged from $170 million to $2 billion, factoring in the company's investment in additional security, and a steep drop in stock price. The damages incurred by those registered network users are a murkier quantity. No major losses have been reported. The theft of that data isn't even confirmed. It could be sitting on a single server somewhere, waiting to be sold off. Or maybe it's already been sliced apart and auctioned off, absorbed into a vast market of stolen financial data. For the 100 million whose accounts were exposed, no closure, or relief, is forthcoming.

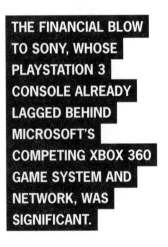

THE FINANCIAL BLOW TO SONY, WHOSE PLAYSTATION 3 CONSOLE ALREADY LAGGED BEHIND MICROSOFT'S COMPETING XBOX 360 GAME SYSTEM AND NETWORK, WAS SIGNIFICANT.

It wasn't the largest data breach in history, but that also occurred recently, when the Heartland Payment credit card system was hacked in 2009, and 140 million credit and debit cards were compromised. What makes 2011 special is the escalation. Suddenly, the attacks came more often, and with a startling rate of success.

At the end of March, two weeks before the Sony intrusion, one of the largest online marketing firms in the world, Dallas-based Epsilon Data Management, was hacked. The compromised data consisted mostly of customer contact lists—names and email addresses—gathered by 2500 clients. Those lists included customers of the biggest names in finance and commerce, from lenders (Capital One, Citigroup, JPMorgan Chase) to chain stores (Best Buy, Kroger, Walgreens) as well as more obscure clients, such as the College Board, which manages the SAT admissions test.

On May 10, 2011, hackers stormed the systems of Citigroup. The firm waited three weeks to announce the attack, giving an obtuse reference to some 200,000 accounts being compromised. Later, it would reveal that the breach extended to more than 360,000 credit cards in North America.

Other attacks throughout the year were smaller in scope, but shared the same prize: customer data. In June, user information was lifted from a forum owned by Electronic Arts, one of the world's largest video game companies. The passwords, email addresses, physical addresses, birth dates and phone numbers of tens of thousands of customers were exposed. And while Sony suffered a string of hacks after bringing its PlayStation Network back online in May, hobbling the service until July, the biggest subsequent attack on the service came in October. An estimated 93,000 member accounts were closed, after a barrage of suspicious log-ins was detected, and countless passwords were stolen.

Within the diversity of targets and attacks was an emergent strategy. Once inside a system, if credit and bank account information wasn't available, hackers stole the data that would help them, or their clients, stage follow-up attacks.

The most effective type of secondary assault is known as spear phishing. A standard phishing attempt might involve blanketing millions of email accounts with urgent, false requests from JPMorgan Chase to log in or click on a link, gambling that some of those messages will arrive at genuine customers of the institution. Spear phishing is more efficient, filtering those millions of anonymous email addresses for specific customers: those with confirmed JPMorgan Chase accounts, or member profiles on the servers of Sony, or Electronic Arts. Now, the odds are better of finding someone willing to unknowingly hand over their log-in data or download a program that watches their keystrokes, effectively handing over access to your account.

We'll parse through all of that (Chapter 9 also covers phishing threats), but the meaning is simple. What's occurring is blunt, and sensationalistic, and inevitable: One way or another, hackers are coming for our money.

HACKING AS A GROWTH INDUSTRY

It's easy to dismiss phishing victims as fools. Who are these marks, too clueless to turn on spam filters, and too naive to recognize the impostor messages that slip through?

The victims aren't as rare, or as hapless as you might expect. Studies have shown that as many as 3 percent of all targets are tricked into taking some sort of action by phishing messages. Spear phishing, on the other hand, reels in 30 percent or more. In a 2010 study conducted by Pittsburgh's Carnegie Mellon University and the Indraprashtra Institute of Information Technology in Delhi, India, roughly one half of all subjects clicked on spear-phishing links. These weren't fleeting deceptions, either—of those tricked into an initial click, 90 percent entered further information. And while received wisdom would single out older users as more vulnerable, the study's results supported past research, finding that 18 to 25-year-olds are still the most susceptible age group.

In 2003, phishing accounted for $1.2 billion in lost funds around the world. Back then, victims typically had to download and possibly run an application that showed up in their inbox. "Email attachments were once the most common vector used by malicious code to infect computers," Marc Fossi, a researcher for Symantec, told *Popular Mechanics* in 2010. "However, various protection measures like email attachment blocking, along with user education about these threats, have limited their effectiveness." So the phishers adapted, largely ditching the attached malicious software, and focusing instead on tempting users with a single unwise click on a link. By the end of 2010, phishing, and the malware that waits at the end of each confidence game, was stealing $10 billion annually.

There are too many types of malware to list comprehensively here— like the viral strains and bacterial invasions they're modeled after, new generations of code follow their predecessors into the wild, mutating and merging in unpredictable ways. There are nuisance programs that regurgitate pop-up windows for a few hours before being expunged. Others might wreak havoc for a week or more, before Microsoft or anti-virus specialists such as Kasperksy and Symantec issue a security update that extracts or bars them from entry. And there are trends in bugs, patterns of abuse tied to the lifecycle of each new version of the dominant operating system, Windows. Always, though, malware grows stronger.

THERE ARE TOO MANY TYPES OF MALWARE TO LIST COMPREHENSIVELY.

Take, for example, keyloggers. These programs record the keystrokes made by a user, including account numbers and passwords, everything needed to take over someone's financial identity. It's an unnerving, but often inefficient method of stealing access, forcing "carders," as stolen account traffickers are known, to scan through browser histories and rambling email missives until a tell-tale jumble of characters pops out of the noise.

Occasionally, however, the man-hours do pay off. In one of the most famous keylogging cases, in 2004 hackers siphoned $90,000 out of Florida businessman Joe Lopez's commercial bank account. Lopez noticed the suspicious wire transfer immediately, and asked Bank of America to freeze the transaction. The bank refused. Soon, the transfer reached Riga, the capital of Latvia, where a stranger withdrew $20,000. The final $70,000 was locked down at the Latvian bank, which refused to reverse the transaction. Bank of America refused as well, denying any responsibility to cover the lost money or credit Lopez's account, after Secret Service agents found a known keylogger program, Coredoor, on his home computer.

According to the bank, Coredoor would have been wiped out by properly updated anti-virus software. The onus was on Lopez to keep his security current. In the end, Lopez sued, forcing an undisclosed settlement out of Bank of America.

That, of course, was a rare find: a keylogging target with significant funds in his account, and a banking institution that simply watched as stolen funds were transferred and withdrawn. At the time, that was the modus operandi—large, occasional withdrawals from a select group of targets.

Today, keylogging software is smarter, and more widespread. "We've seen this progression over the last six years ago or so, from keyloggers grabbing everything that the target was typing, to malware that is much more specific," says Roel Schouwenberg, Senior Malware Researcher at Kaspersky Lab. "Now, it might only grab keystrokes when on a secure Web site or on a banking Web site that it knows," says Schouwenberg. While business accounts are still a target, keyloggers now routinely invade consumer accounts, withdrawing $10,000 or $15,000 before the customer or financial institution catches on.

The expansion in targets, from big fish to small, medium, and every other size and stripe of fish, is a sign of a flourishing industry. Once upon a time, scammers were stuck playing at confidence schemes, pretending to be officials of various African countries' governments and begging advanced fees for some make-believe future cash transfer. (Not that the classics don't still work: Those "419" scams, named after the part of the Nigerian Criminal Code that outlaws fraud, hooked U.S. citizens for $720 million in 2005 alone. Much to the government's chagrin, the scam today represents Nigeria's largest source of foreign revenue after oil.) But hacking is no longer just a subculture of disgruntled high school and college students innovating their way into ivory towers—it's a business with revenues of more than $1 trillion a year, according to Norton AntiVirus. Cybercrime syndicates now feature Mafia-like hierarchies, according to the FBI, rapidly making them the agency's top law-enforcement priority. Hacking is now a fulltime criminal profession.

CYBERCRIME SYNDICATES NOW FEATURE MAFIA-LIKE HIERARCHIES, ACCORDING TO THE FBI, RAPIDLY MAKING THEM THE AGENCY'S TOP LAW-ENFORCEMENT PRIORITY.

Today, one of the most commonly used programs for stealing login data is the ZeuS banking Trojan horse. It isn't freeware, traded on forums to sow chaos and comeuppance. ZeuS is a product, albeit an illicit, privately sold product, updated as regularly as other software, and priced at between $3,000 and $4,000 for the standard suite of applications, with additional features costing as much as $20,000. In its current, fully loaded form, ZeuS is a tremendously sophisticated tool, able to send account names, numbers and passwords entered into secure browser windows to a remote party. If necessary, it can simply assume control of an infected computer. Most ZeuS targets become part of colossal botnets, networks of compromised PCs whose pilfered data flows into one centralized set of files, and that can be activated en masse to pump out new waves of Trojan-loaded spam.

Everything ZeuS does is meant to create new products. Logs of stolen data are advertised and sold online. The botnets themselves are up for sale, too, as the complete, secret control of thousands of computers changes hands like any other commodity. So the weak-hearted can cash in early, and pass the risks associated with more serious crimes to their buyers. Or, ZeuS can be a one-stop shop, empowering a group of hackers to rob the accounts they've gained access to.

The true impact of ZeuS is difficult to determine—estimates of total infections ranged from 3.6 million computers in 2009, to as many as 13 million by early 2012. The occasional arrest of ZeuS gangs provides another sense of scale. In March, Microsoft employees joined U.S. Marshals to raid hosting centers in Lombard, Illinois, and Scranton, Pennsylvania, seizing servers the gang members had used to command and control the botnet. The software giant became part of the takedown after pulling a clever legal maneuver: Microsoft sued the crime ring and was issued a warrant to seize the servers thanks to the Racketeer Influenced and Corrupt Organizations, or RICO, Act—the same one long used by federal prosecutors to target the mafia. Microsoft's civil complaint accused 39 "John Does" of "controlling computer botnets thereby injuring plaintiffs, and their customers and members." Over the past five years, Microsoft alleged, the crime ring had stolen over $100 million.

Following initial arrests of some members of the ZeuS mafia in 2010, when the tally was a relatively paltry $3 million stolen from dozens of bank accounts in the U.S., Manhattan District Attorney Cyrus Vance, Jr. told reporters at a press conference that, "This advanced cybercrime ring is a disturbing example of organized crime in the 21st century—high tech and widespread. The 36 defendants indicted by our office stole from ordinary citizens and businesses using keyboards— not a gun."

To date, dozens of hackers and their accomplices have been convicted on both sides of the Atlantic, in connection with that single ZeuS-based operation. But the ZeuS Trojan rides on—by 2011, it had shapeshifted onto smartphones, and into Facebook friend requests. Using a technique called polymorphic encryption to re-configure itself during new infections, ZeuS prevents—or at least delays—detection by anti-virus software.

ZeuS isn't the only polymorph riding a growing tide of phishing and spear-phishing email blasts—anti-virus software-makers Symantec spotted a surge in polymorphic encryption in the summer of 2011, which accounted for 23.7 percent of all email-carried malware in July, and 72 percent by September. ZeuS is also just one product in a growth industry of hacks made simple, or hacking-for-fire. "There are open source communities where you can create attacks from

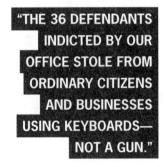

"THE 36 DEFENDANTS INDICTED BY OUR OFFICE STOLE FROM ORDINARY CITIZENS AND BUSINESSES USING KEYBOARDS— NOT A GUN."

pre-existing components, fitting them together like LEGO© blocks," says Adrian Turner, CEO of security firm Mocana. "There are marketplaces where you can pay money to have a certain type of attack built or developed for you."

Whether home-built or outsourced, account-cracking malware is more common than ever, more invasive, and harder to defend against. It's carried to fresh victims by a never-ending torrent of phishing and spear-phishing emails. Some are sent at random, but victims of data breaches become the highest-priority targets for those messages, since they're more likely to fall for one of the countless scams flooding their inboxes. This is what hacking has become. What may have been a novelty act in the 1980s has become almost unrecognizable, part of an ecosystem of electronic theft, with food chains composed entirely of stolen, sold and resold data.

LAUGHING AT SECURITY—AND PRIVACY

To be fair, some hackers aren't profiting from their crimes. There are true believers out there, like the aggressively old-fashioned crew that took credit for some of the most infamous attacks in 2011, including at least one major intrusion at Sony.

That group, which called itself Lulz Security, or LulzSec (internet shorthand for laughing out loud at computer security), was an offshoot of the headline grabbing band of hackers known as "Anonymous." LulzSec summed up its *raison d'être* in an online announcement on June 25, 2011 saying that its six members were disbanding.

"For the past 50 days we've been disrupting and exposing corporations, governments, often the general population itself, and quite possibly everything in between, just because we could," the post read. Over the course of what it called "50 Days of Lulz," the group had taken credit for a string of attacks on various kinds of targets, the biggest of which was Sony Pictures. LulzSec claimed to have stolen more than a million user passwords, names, addresses, email addresses, and posted samples online as proof. Data from tens of thousands of users were exposed elsewhere, includes accounts from a pornography site, as well as the United

States Senate's official site. At other times, the group launched less-sophisticated, brute-force temporary takedowns of Web sites belonging to the CIA and the Arizona Department of Public Safety.

In its farewell post, LulzSec calls for others to continue its antisecurity campaign, hoping to foment a full-scale revolution. "Together, united, we can stomp down our common oppressors and imbue ourselves with the power and freedom we deserve."

Before vanishing, LulzSec released its final trove of plundered data: 750,000 accounts, many of them taken from videogame forums and services.

As finales go, it revealed more about LulzSec than any of the group's scattered public comments. In its self-professed ideology, LulzSec was returning to hacking's iconoclastic roots. It struck out at corporations for their greed, at the government for its anti-immigration policies and increased focus on cyberattacks, and at nonprofits, such as PBS, because of its negative characterization of hackers. LulzSec also played the classic, almost mythical role of the charitable hacker, penetrating some systems without exposing data, as a sincere warning to its victims to beef up security, before the real villains came charging in. "Please fix your junk, thanks! ^_^" the group tweeted, after breaking into a major videogame studio's system, and refraining from posting some 20,000 compromised user accounts.

LULZSEC CLAIMED TO HAVE STOLEN MORE THAN A MILLION USER PASSWORDS, NAMES, ADDRESSES, EMAIL ADDRESSES, AND POSTED SAMPLES ONLINE AS PROOF.

But LulzSec was not a coherent, populist guerrilla movement. For every group of users it claimed to protect, it offered a different data dump of exposed accounts. A few thousand pieces of personally identifiable information (PII) here, another 62,000 users there, culminating in that final cache of 750,000 accounts.

And in so doing, LulzSec, and groups and individuals like them, feed a far more vicious class of predator. The ecosystem of persistent digital assault, always prodding users for vulnerabilities and financial institutions for security exploits, feeds on this steady supply of privacy violations. Compromised accounts drift like kelp in open waters. PII betrays its subjects, and leads to more PII, which is compiled into databases. All of the principles we've covered so far—the growing amount of data, the greater ease with which it can be collected, how it's filtered and organized, resold, reused, becoming a new form of transferable currency—are at play here. The only difference is the raw illegality of attacks on financial privacy. None of the aggressors claim to be honest brokers.

GROUPS LIKE LULZSEC POSE AS KEEPERS OF THE FLAME, SOWING ANARCHY BECAUSE THEY CAN, AND BECAUSE IT'S NECESSARY.

Some, however, are delusional. Groups like LulzSec pose as keepers of the flame, sowing anarchy because they can, and because it's necessary. What they can't face is what's changed, the grotesque form hacking has taken, and the consequences of their pranks. They pass fresh targets to a criminal enterprise that drains billions from the global economy, and millions from average people, and call it tough love. They are oblivious to the state of panic they support.

Five members of LulzSec, however, have learned about the consequences of breached privacy the hard way. In March, the five hackers' homes in England, Scotland, Ireland and Chicago were raided in near-simultaneous assaults by law enforcement agents—who were aided by none other than the de facto leader of the group. Hector Xavier Monsegur, an unemployed 28-year-old living on New York's Lower East Side, had been secretly busted by the FBI nine months earlier and charged with conspiracy to engage in computer hacking, conspiracy to commit bank fraud and aggravated identity theft. Facing 122 years in prison, "Sabu," as he was known to the LulzSec hacker cell he oversaw, rolled over on all of them. "Since literally the day he was arrested, the defendant has been cooperating with the government proactively," the assistant U.S. attorney told a New York judge during a secret court session held soon after Monsegur's arrest. "The defendant has literally worked around the clock with federal agents. He has been staying up sometimes all night engaging in conversations with co-conspirators that are helping the government to build cases against those co-conspirators."

It seems privacy's loss is always a shock, even to those who dedicate their lives to ending it.

CHAPTER 7

WHO'S SPYING ON YOUR DNA

SHE GOES BY THE UNWIELDY USERNAME POGOWASRIGHT. This is the only name she'll share. Talking via Skype, Pogo claims to be a licensed mental heath care professional in New York City, and a published author. It's too risky to reveal her identity, she explains—she wants to keep her practice and patients isolated from her mission.

That mission is to expose and publicize the daily data breaches occurring across the country. On a trio of websites—Databreaches.net, PHIprivacy.net, and PogoWasRight.org—she files news items, and compiles a growing database of those breaches. The list is comprehensive, and staggering.

December 2010: Backup tapes are stolen from a data management company's unlocked van. The lost data includes the names, Social

Security numbers, addresses, and health information of 1.7 million patients and employees of a Bronx, New York hospital.

March 2011: Nine servers go missing from a data center in Rancho Cordova, California. The personal, financial, and health information of 1.9 million current and former members of Health Net's health insurance plans are among the missing data.

There are hundreds more, many of them too small to be picked up by local news outlets, others that made headlines but quickly disappeared, with no additional leads or developments to report on. Pogo reports on all forms of data breaches, from reports of credit-card skimming to server hackers. But health-related information hits closer to home. "All healthcare professionals are really concerned about patient confidentiality and privacy. But if you're a mental heath professional, you're dealing with seriously stigmatizing stuff," she says.

Along with gathering reports and statistics, Pogo has discovered major breaches before they reached the media. In 2008, she was tipped off about the insurance provider Wellpoint, Inc., and the fact that its members' personal information was accessible online, without a password. At the time, the breach seemed to affect at least 100,000 people. She claims to have notified Wellpoint in April, asking them to secure the servers, or else she would go public with the story. Wellpoint's response was not positive. Almost simultaneously, Pogo released her report, and Wellpoint approached the Associated Press with its side of the story.

ALONG WITH GATHERING REPORTS AND STATISTICS, POGO HAS DISCOVERED MAJOR BREACHES BEFORE THEY REACHED THE MEDIA.

Two months later, Wellpoint was fined $100,000 by the state of Indiana, for failing to report to its members that its servers had been compromised by hackers, and that some 1,000,000 records, related to roughly 130,000 people, had been exposed online. That information had been accessible to anyone with the proper URLs since 2007. "Think about it, over a million records sitting on the internet for over a year," Pogo says. "Now if someone has a cancer treatment drug, or arthritis medication, or antidepressants, that's out in the open," Pogo says. "Everybody has something to hide, even if it's not socially stigmatizing."

Pogo isn't alone. There are less shadowy breach-watchers, non-profit organizations like Privacy Clearing House and the Identity Theft Resource Center. The totality of their findings is punishing, a litany of Social Security Numbers left unshredded in dumpsters, laptops and servers stolen or hacked. If Pogo is telling the truth, though, about her acts of borderline vigilantism—she points to online, dated archives of her April 2008 Wellpoint coverage as evidence that she beat the media to the punch—there might be hope. The hemorrhage of data from hospitals, health insurers and pharmacies isn't some futuristic menace. It's a present-day reality, one that she's wrestling into the light, by any means necessary.

OUT FOR BLOOD

For Gary Avary, the breach of privacy was more personal than a faceless hack or theft, and more visceral.

What they wanted was his blood—seven vials of it, he claims. This was December 2000, three months after Avary, a maintenance worker for Burlington Northern Santa Fe (BNSF) railroad, had been diagnosed with carpal tunnel syndrome. His median nerve, which connects the wrist to his hand, had become pinched, causing pain and numbness in his fingers. Repetitive motion is the main cause of carpal tunnel syndrome, though extremes of temperature can contribute. As a trackman, replacing torn rail lines after derailments, or conducting routine maintenance, always with an array of power tools, exposed to the elements for most of it, Avary was a model victim. It was no surprise when BNSF approved his surgery. In an industry like rail, carpal tunnel disability claims aren't exactly rare.

Blood tests, on the other hand, seemed out of place. Avary refused. Reportedly, a disciplinary meeting followed. Avary then contacted his union lawyer, who contacted the government. From there, everything unraveled.

According to a lawsuit filed by the Equal Employment Opportunity Commission (EEOC), BNSF had come up with a scheme. What if there was another reason so many of its workers were suffering from carpal tunnel syndrome, something that predated their employment? Something that, in fact, was there from birth, woven into the proteins of their DNA?

BNSF wanted Avary's blood, and the blood of dozens of other employee, to test for missing chromosomes. More specifically, genetic material found to be missing from chromosome 17. It's an aberration that can lead to a host of conditions. One of those is hereditary neuropathy with liability to pressure palsies (HNPP), a nervous disorder that can result in numbness in the limbs and extremities, and severe loss of motor control. Sufferers may also be more prone to carpal tunnel syndrome.

WHAT IF THERE WAS ANOTHER REASON SO MANY OF ITS WORKERS WERE SUFFERING FROM CARPAL TUNNEL SYNDROME, SOMETHING THAT PREDATED THEIR EMPLOYMENT?

BNSF conducted genetic testing on its workers, without their consent or notification in the slim hope that some of the 125 or so employees who had developed carpal tunnel during 2000 might be missing portions of chromosome 17. If those workers were found to have the genetic condition, BNSF presumably would have argued that the mutation was responsible for the workers' carpal tunnel, not the work itself.

88

In fact, Avary was lucky. In his Congressional testimony, Avary claimed that his wife, Janice, a registered nurse, learned of the genetic dimension of the mandatory medical test through a slip-up in conversation with BNSF's medical liaison officer. Soon after, the EEOC was suing BNSF for violating the Americans with Disabilities Act, which prohibits businesses from discriminating against employees because of disabilities. The terms of BNSF's settlement with the federal government throw the precise details into question—despite paying $2.2 million in damages to 36 employees, the company disputes much of what it's accused of, including reports that it disciplined workers who refused to give blood.

For BNSF, the timing could not have been worse. Days after it was sued by the EEOC, government-funded geneticists released the first detailed, plain-text analysis of the human genome, which they called *The Book of Life*. The world appeared to be at a thrilling, but terrifying crossroads. A full reckoning of our DNA could herald targeted drug treatments, or even preemptive ones, based on genetic predispositions toward one disease or another. But this was intimate knowledge. It could expose conditions that patients weren't ready or willing to reveal. In theory, every built-in biological frailty could be teased from a sample of blood or spit, and inform discussions and decisions by strangers. As the national media grappled with the significance of *The Book of Life*, BNSF's testing was proof that genetic discrimination wasn't a long-term threat. It was already at work.

So the concept of genetic privacy was introduced, at the precise moment that it had been publicly violated. But BNSF's blunder runs much deeper than a simple matter of intrusion. What the company was

89

searching for—evidence of pre-existing conditions—revealed a larger, more widespread privacy threat. What if the seekers aren't revealing hidden truths at all? What if the clues they're gathering are meaningless, and the conclusions drawn are wrong?

THE TROUBLE WITH DATA

"For many people, the biggest concerns about privacy aren't about the data itself. They're about the ways people could misuse data to hurt you, to discriminate against you," says Deven McGraw, director of the Health Privacy Project at the Center for Democracy and Technology.

In BNSF's case, the problem started at the beginning, with the decision to zero in on HNPP. It's an extremely rare condition, showing up in as many as one out of 20,000 people, and most commonly surfacing during childhood or adolescence. BNSF's total workforce numbered 39,000. Roughly 120 of its employees had filed carpal tunnel syndrome claims in 2001, nearly three dozen of whom were later identified as having been genetically tested.

Set aside, for a moment, everything but the numbers. If you assume that a randomly selected group of 39,000 people might include, on average, two sufferers of hereditary neuropathy, then BNSF was violating the genetic privacy of 35 people in order to find that troublesome duo. Never mind that someone whose nerves are hyper-sensitive to pressure, who experiences intermittent waves pain and numbness, would be unlikely to gravitate towards the hard, hands-on physical work of rail repair.

And it gets worse. Detecting that a subject is missing a portion of chromosome 17 might seem to indicate the presence of HNPP. But it might also lead to suspicions that he or she is suffering from a range of issues, such as leukemia, abnormal brain development, and various obscure nervous disorders, some of which can lead to paralysis. It would be genetic profiling, in other words, and like all forms of profiling, it would open the door to more breaches, and more evidence that proves nothing. That's the best-case scenario. BNSF's motives and reasoning aren't the stuff of shadowy, all-knowing megacorporations. They are blunders that don't survive scrutiny of any kind. Which is why they're so frightening.

THE RISE OF PERSONAL GENOMICS

Privacy breaches are not always smart. Sometimes, as in BNSF's genetic testing, they are ill-conceived, and inflict no tangible injuries. None of the tested employees were denied health coverage, or accused of hiding a pre-existing condition. Testing was halted, and BNSF settled the case. From that win came a larger victory, when Congress passed the Genetic Information Nondiscrimination Act (GINA) in 2008, which prohibits employers and health insurers from basing human resources or coverage-related decisions based on genetic data. In conjunction with 1996's Health Insurance Portability and Accountability Act (HIPPA), which regulates how personal health information can be shared by insurers and providers, the gates to genetic privacy seemed secure.

But in the ensuing years, legislation has proven a poor defense against mounting threats. It's not that the courts are filled with cases of genetic or medical discrimination. Rather, the violations flow around GINA and HIPAA, laws that are necessarily narrow in their breadth and powers, and unable to adapt to the pace of technology. And those violations, like so many privacy threats, are often hard to confirm or even define. In part, that's because the biggest breaches have yet to happen, or at least have yet to be exposed.

Take, for example, the rise of private genetic sequencing services, such as 23andMe, which for a small fee will analyze a "snip" of a customer's DNA. This is not a full-genome analysis, which would take months and cost hundreds of thousands, but a quick and dirty look at a limited amount of genetic material. 23andMe then reports back with two distinct types of educated guesses: the illnesses you're predisposed to develop, and clues about your biological ancestors, such as their ethnicity, and where they may have lived.

Whether it's a wise decision to learn your susceptibility to various crippling and terminal diseases is a separate debate—23andMe offers a voluntary, paid service.

However, it also sells its collected genetic data to third parties. In 23andMe's defense, the buyers appear to be research organizations, and the company requires user consent, not through obscure privacy policies, but direct requests that highlight the lack of useful genetic data available to researchers. Sharing your data is framed as a charitable donation, a small contribution to the greater scientific good.

SHARING YOUR DATA IS FRAMED AS A CHARITABLE DONATION, A SMALL CONTRIBUTION TO THE GREATER SCIENTIFIC GOOD.

23andMe collects its own, unspecified fees, and your genetic information is presumably stripped of its identifying characteristics, packed up with other generous donations, and sent along its altruistic way.

To see some sort of menace in that transaction requires a healthy dose of paranoia. Or, perhaps, another refresher on data's lack of loyalty, that tendency to spill all secrets, and snitch on anyone.

THE REFINEMENT OF REIDENTIFICATION

The sequencing results that are resold by 23andMe are anonymized. This is a widespread answer to privacy concerns. It involves a kind of encryption, where data is stripped of anything that would identify its subject, such as names and addresses. Instead of handing over a full profile of someone at risk of developing Parkinson's, 23andMe delivers a bundle of genetic characteristics, some of which point to some unnamed, unidentified person's predisposition toward that disease.

But just as methods of encryption beget techniques of decryption, anonymized data have a natural enemy—reidentification. With access to enough data points, a diligent mathematician or computer scientist can theoretically connect the dots, filling in the intentionally missing gaps, and reconstructing the ejected personal information.

In 2007, University of Texas computer scientists Arvind Narayanan and Vitaly Shmatikov demonstrated why re-identification is everyone's problem. At the time, DVD rent-by-mail service Netflix held an ongoing contest, offering $1 million to the first team that could beat the accuracy of its recommendation algorithm by 10 percent. Since Neflix's existing code suggested DVDs based on a submitted ratings, the company released more than a hundred million of those ratings, as submitted by roughly 480,000 members. Narayanan and Shmatikov took the provided dataset, and with a minimal amount of additional information, such as when a given user may have watched a handful of movies, and what ratings he or she assigned, drew a host of conclusions about its anonymous subjects. The team's algorithm could compile a com-

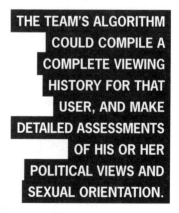

THE TEAM'S ALGORITHM COULD COMPILE A COMPLETE VIEWING HISTORY FOR THAT USER, AND MAKE DETAILED ASSESSMENTS OF HIS OR HER POLITICAL VIEWS AND SEXUAL ORIENTATION.

plete viewing history for that user, and make detailed assessments of his or her political views and sexual orientation. Those Netflix members who had also rated even a few films on the Internet Movie Database, where profiles are public, could be fully identified, stripping away all pretenses of anonymity.

The stakes, at first glance, appear awfully low. The chances of anyone taking the time to out their associates by way of Netflix are beyond slim. What caught the attention of privacy experts was how little data was needed to uniquely identify hundreds of thousands of strangers. When Narayanan and Shmatikov published their findings in 2008, the promise of anonymized data would never be the same.

"It was a tsunami in my world," says the Electronic Frontier Foundation's Lee Tien. "We thought we understood the importance of reidentification before that. Once we saw that paper, everyone went, 'Oh shit.' It means all of the existing databases are this amazing wealth of reindentifable info."

The raw materials for reidentification are everywhere, it turns out. The trick is to merge seemingly disparate data points, with each bit of information ruling out whole populations, until the algorithm is left with its best guess. With nothing but an unnamed subject's zip code, for example, there's no hope of plucking one person's identity out of hundreds or thousands. Add gender, however, and that sample is cut in half. Throw in age, and suddenly something scary happens. With those three bits of information, 87 percent of Americans can be uniquely identified.

As far back as 1997, Carnegie Mellon University computer science professor Latanya Sweeney (the guru behind the 87 percent figure) showed its implications for the healthcare industry—and your privacy. While a doctoral student at MIT, Sweeney began scouring records for the Group Insurance Commission, which purchases health insurance for Massachusetts state employees. Because the data was stripped of names, addresses and social security numbers, and thus believed to be anonymous, GIC gave their records to researchers and sold a copy to the healthcare industry. Sweeney, however, cross-referenced those records with the simple Cambridge voter registration list, which she purchased for $20. From GIC's list of 135,000 records, she checked one particular birth date: July 31, 1945. That narrowed the list to six voters, only three of whom were men. She then factored in the zip code 02138. And just like that, the graduate student identified the medical records of William Weld—then the governor of Massachusetts, and the man who had publicly insisted the patients' data was completely protected.

> THAT NARROWED THE LIST TO SIX VOTERS, ONLY THREE OF WHOM WERE MEN. SHE THEN FACTORED IN THE ZIP CODE 02138.

DETACHING THE DATA POINTS

Which brings us back to genetic information. In some cases, reidentification can be thwarted by not only scrambling or removing the subject's identity, but tearing the data apart. A roster of Alcoholics Anonymous members that includes ages and genders is just waiting to be lined up with additional data points, such as license plate numbers pulled from a specific red light camera. Two lists, on the other hand, the first listing ages and the second showing a simple ratio of males to females, lose their value as unique identifiers. In this way, demographic statistics about a local AA chapter could be extracted, with minimal risk of personal exposure.

Unfortunately, not all data points are so easily detached. Since most gene sequences consist of a string of letters, and nothing more, any reorganization would destroy their utility, turning a sample into a random, possibly misleading jumble of A's, C's, G's, and Ts. This is information that can't be sliced into smaller portions and fed into a larger, aggregate collection. The snips are intact, and waiting to be cross-referenced with other data points. If 23andMe's financial records were hacked or subpoenaed, merging those databases would be child's play, names sliding easily into place above estimates of each customer's doomsday or undiagnosed conditions. And the sequences hold their own clues, guesses at where the user most likely lives, where his or her parents were born, what his or her ethnicity is.

This isn't quite as hypothetical as it seems. At the end of 2011, Google shuttered its Google Health service, which allowed users to load their medical information into the company's servers and grant access to specific, trusted physicians. The service had come under fire, for anonymizing its users' data, and mining it for various purposes. The risk of reidentification, the critics argued, outweighed the potential benefits. (Microsoft's rival program, HealthVault, which currently allows its millions of users to log in with their Facebook credentials—"It's important to note that this does

THE RISK OF REIDENTIFICATION, THE CRITICS ARGUED, OUTWEIGHED THE POTENTIAL BENEFITS.

not mean that HealthVault information will show up on your (Facebook) 'wall!'" Microsoft insists—is still going strong.)

Of course, that reidentification potential extends to nearly every form of data collection—but the idea of outsiders spying on our health strikes at the heart of privacy concerns. The chance that online tracking cookies could be used to single out a specific person was one reason Narayanan began working on the Do Not Track browser. The Federal Trade Commission agrees, citing reidentification as one major reason there must be limits on online tracking. Who might be monitoring those web searches to identify a nuisance bug bite? Or a sexual problem? How might that be coupled with other data points that can be collected—like the general geographic location provided by an IP address?

The danger, experts agree, has less to do with the present than the future, when making connections in the swelling pool of data will be less labor-intensive, and increasingly automated. It was this fear that propelled the issue of reidentification to the United States Supreme

Court in April 2011. Though it would reveal itself to be an intricate case, the facts of Sorrel v. IMS Health inc. exposed the myth, and the oxymoron, of health privacy.

THE LETTER OF THE ETHICS

First, a bit of background: By law, pharmacies must keep a record of the prescriptions picked up by their customers. It's a simple requirement, intended to prevent the shady, excessive dispensing of drugs. But as the great American data rush forges on, drug stores are cashing in, selling those prescription drug histories—including the name of each patient's prescribing doctor, as well as the recipients' age, gender, and the time and location of each filled prescription—to data vendors, who make some vague effort to strip a patient's identifiable data before reselling the records to pharmaceutical companies. Drug firms want the information so they can better market specific drugs to individual doctors who might be prescribing a generic or competitor's product.

This three-step dance is perfectly legal because drug vendors anonymize customers' names, replacing them with seemingly random strings of characters. Or it was legal, until Vermont passed a law in 2011 that banned the use of prescription records for marketing purposes—effectively, making it illegal for pharmacies to do the first step, and drug companies to do the third step—classifying it as an unfair business practice. Three data vendors at the heart of the second step, Verispan, IMS Health and SDI, sued, claiming their free speech had been violated.

The case of Sorrel v. IMS Health reached the Supreme Court in 2011, where the details of this relatively unknown, and arguably sordid arrangement were laid bare. But the biggest revelation was how the prescription histories were anonymized, and how they weren't.

While the names on those pharmacy records were replaced, thanks to Sweeney's work 14 years earlier observers knew the information that was sold allowed for nearly instant reidentification. Those records also providing a wealth of additional data points about customers. In fact, one of the data vendors' employees testified that his company alone tracked some 200 million people. And while Verispan, IMS Health and SDI never attached specific names to those hundreds of millions of patients, they had no qualms about violating their privacy, and found creative ways to do so. The vendors would match a given patient's answers to marketing surveys to the rest of their profile, for instance, hoping to find out what was discussed during doctor's visits. "If you don't know what doctors are saying to their patients, you're missing part of the story," the Verispan employee explained in court.

> THERE'S NOTHING PREVENTING DATA VENDORS FROM RESELLING DATA TO OTHER CUSTOMERS, AND OTHER VENDORS, ALL OF WHOM CAN RESELL THEM ONCE MORE.

Privacy groups, not surprisingly, threw their support behind Vermont, decrying both the admitted breaches and the fact that such easily reidentifiable data was being sold to third parties. After all, there's nothing preventing data vendors from reselling data to other customers, and other vendors, all of whom can resell them once more, until these records have propagated throughout multiple industries and onto untold numbers of servers. What happens when one or more of these companies files for bankruptcy, and begins selling off its assets to even less scrupulous organizations?

Worse still was that the data history itself—unlike an email address or credit card information—can't be issued a new password or account number. The data compiled described years of prescriptions, along with glimpses behind the veil of doctor-patient confidentiality. And compounding the issue, to the naked—or unscrupulous—eye, that prescription history could be misleading: Valtrex could have been briefly prescribed for a suspected case of herpes, followed by a later, undocumented diagnosis of a less chronic or stigmatized condition. Mental health prescriptions can be even more confusing, as doctors cycle through an array of drugs, each with its own associated conditions, before settling on a more stable, effective cocktail. A one-time prescription of antipsychotics, for example, might imply schizophrenia, despite an actual diagnosis of depression. The records were a power keg of potential embarrassment or scandal, discussions of life and death, all of it up for sale.

From an ethical standpoint, the data vendors had no defense. Despite arguing that data-mining had become a fact of life in an increasingly data-driven society, they were in a freefall. The details were simply too deplorable.

But the Supreme Court decides matters of law, not ethics. And while the state of Vermont had emphasized privacy and reidentification in its arguments, the case came down to a specific legal point—whether the government had the right to ban the use of prescription record datamining, because it helped drugmakers combat the popularity of generic versions of their products. In that light, the state's case fell flat.

"SERIOUS AND UNRESOLVED ISSUES"

The court ruled in favor of the vendors, six to three. Vermont's ruling was reversed, and the right to buy and sell this particular data was once again legal. Justice Anthony Kennedy recognized the potential privacy conflicts in the majority opinion, writing that mining and otherwise gathering data in automated processes could represent "serious and unresolved issues with respect to personal privacy and the dignity it seeks to secure." That threat was deemed irrelevant, however, a matter for another case.

The defining health privacy showdown, in other words, has yet to reach the highest court. The same could be said for nearly every other aspect of data privacy. What's often missing is clear evidence of widespread abuse, of laws broken, of damages incurred and lives ruined.

Until something more tangible than ominous foreshadowing arrives, the Supreme Court is powerless to enact sweeping changes. The right to privacy—even of our most personal information—remains a scattered assemblage of narrow protections. The data, meanwhile, continues to flow, and collect, and merge, creating a form from the chaos. All privacy threats are, ultimately, about reidentification—yet every moment of assumed anonymity can be exposed, every data point used to reconstruct a larger scene. With enough of them, observers can paint a detailed picture of no less than our own bodies.

THE DEFINING HEALTH PRIVACY SHOWDOWN, IN OTHER WORDS, HAS YET TO REACH THE HIGHEST COURT.

In many ways, health privacy is a last stand. Genetic information is the most unique identifier of all. Others might share your age or name or gender, possibly the same zip code. No one shares your exact genetic code. And those who share some of your DNA also share the risk. "What makes genetic data different, is that people look at its predictive capability, and not just about you," says the Center for Democracy and Technology's Deven McGraw. "If I get a genetic test that indicates I have predisposition towards a disorder, it implicates my family members, even if they were never tested."

Genetic data flows backwards, too, hinting at your ancestors' health, at their origins and ethnicity. It is among the easiest data to reidentify.

And yet, genetic data collects on the servers of companies like 23andMe, on researchers' laptops, and in online cloud computing storage services. It may take a subpoena, or hack, or less-sophisticated breach to spark the most explosive privacy battle of all.

Or it could be good intentions. In late 2011, Google partnered with genetic data management firm DNAnexus to take over the hosting of the world's largest collection of whole-genome information. The goal was to make that data entirely web-accessible, allowing researchers to search and browse a huge archive of publicly available DNA data from the cloud. It will be free for researchers. It could fuel countless break-throughs across the entire, varied spectrum of genomics research.

Naturally, the genetic data is available for download from any browser.

CHAPTER 8

WHO'S SPYING ON YOUR KIDS

THE STORY OF PRIVACY, and its dismantling, is not a story. It's too fractured, too messy. There is no beginning, no moment before the battles were first fought, and no end to the rising drum beat of persistent, systematic intrusions. It lacks the villains of a ripping narrative, littered instead with distant nations of faceless hackers, lobbying blocks of blameless marketers, and the occasional overly patriotic officer of the law. It's a litany of oversight, of arrogance, of self-interest, and of accidents, most of them unhappy.

That's one perspective. It implies that there were halcyon days, when every shut door was a bank vault spun tight. It suggests that before GPS trackers, wire taps and malware, that gossip had never shattered lives, that trusts had never been betrayed. It assumes there was a paradise once, that technology somehow lost.

But the story of privacy is not a history of loss. It's about the price of gain. It's about the way we organize information, and the consequences of living in a world where data have jumped the rails, no longer bound by speech, or print, or electrons fired across cables and airspace. Data permeates everything, and its manipulation can seem limitless, unknowable, verging on sorcery. It's difficult to stay rational, to react with anything but paralytic fear.

And then our children's data are exposed, and everything goes to hell.

NEWS OF THE WRETCHED

Three days after 13-year-old Milly Dowler went missing on the way back from her school in southeastern England, there was cause for hope. By then, Dowler's mother, Sally, and father, Bob, had already grown accustomed to calling their daughter's cell phone, and hearing an automated response that the voicemail inbox was full. On March 24, 2002, without explanation, the error message was gone. Someone had deleted the messages. "And it clicked through onto her voicemail, so I heard her voice," Sally Fowler said during a 2011 government inquiry ordered by Britain's Prime Minister. "It was just like, I jumped: She's picked up her voicemails, Bob! She's alive!"

What followed was the opposite of hope—dead ends and fruitless searches. Six months later, a pair of mushroom pickers found Milly Dowler's body in a park roughly 25 miles from where she was last seen alive. Her remains had apparently been pulled from a shallow grave by animals, and scattered. The phone, along with the rest of her belongings, was never recovered. The sign of life in those deleted messages had been fleeting, or false.

Nine years later, the British press was in the first throes of a feeding frenzy, as the *News of the World* (NoW), an influential tabloid owned by the News Corporation, stood accused of hacking into the phones of various public figures. The goal was to intercept voicemail, and chase down whatever ill-gotten leads they contained. By the summer of 2011, it was a juicy, gossipy good time, as a driving force in British culture found itself paying settlements to the likes of actress Sienna Miller, and begging forgiveness for snooping on members of the royal household. An attempt to shift the blame to a small group of unscrupulous editors, and the private detective they had contracted to carry out the hacks, seemed well in hand.

On July 4, the *Guardian* revealed another high-profile victim of *NoW's* illegal phone-hacking campaign. The daily newspaper reported that in the days and weeks after the teenager disappeared, Milly Dowler's voicemail was monitored by the tabloid. The deleted messages, according to the *Guardian*, had likely been intentionally cleared to make room for more incoming voicemail, or accidentally wiped. That false hope had been the wake left by sharks.

What was a public outcry became a howl, and grew louder in the next few days, as advertisers abandoned the Sunday tabloid en masse. New reports surfaced that *NoW* had hacked phones belonging to parents whose two 10-year-old daughters had also been abducted and killed. Other accusations followed in rapid succession, that the hacks included the relatives of soldiers killed in Afghanistan, and family members of victims of the 2005 London bombings. Prime Minister David Cameron called the intrusions "absolutely disgust-

THE DAILY NEWSPAPER REPORTED THAT IN THE DAYS AND WEEKS AFTER THE TEENAGER DISAPPEARED, MILLY DOWLER'S VOICEMAIL WAS MONITORED BY THE TABLOID.

ing." "We are no longer talking here about politicians and celebrities," he told the House of Commons. "We are talking about murder victims, potentially terrorist victims, having their phones hacked into."

On July 10, less than a week after the *Guardian* ran its front-page story on Dowler, the *News of the World* printed its final edition. The 168-year-old tabloid shut down immediately, and more than a dozen of its editors and executives would face criminal charges. A bid by News Corp. CEO Rupert Murdoch to purchase a British TV network was scuttled, and the company's shares tumbled. Since then, the mogul's own sons have come under fire, with at least one of them, James, tied directly to the phone hacks. James Murdoch ultimately resigned his posts with his father's newspaper business, and then with the BSkyB satellite broadcasting company owned by News Corporation, in early 2012.

To credit the Dowler hack with the fall of *NoW* would be simplifying things. But not by much. Once the tabloid was blamed for willfully violating the privacy of a murdered teenager, the end came quickly. Threats to privacy occur every moment of every day, some of them impacting millions at a time, with no penalties or consequences for those responsible. This was different. It was a child. It was repulsive. It doesn't get any simpler.

THE POWER OF PANIC

But what if there was no proof that *NoW* had deleted those messages, triggering that heart-breaking response from Dowler's parents, and eventually putting a tragic face to an otherwise impersonal scandal?

On December 13, 2011, the *Guardian* was forced to retract its accusation, writing in the paper's corrections column that new evidence "led the Metropolitan police to believe that this was unlikely to have been correct and that while the *News of the World* hacked Milly Dowler's phone the newspaper is unlikely to have been responsible for the deletion of a set of voicemails from the phone that caused her parents to have false hopes that she was alive..."

The messages were most likely wiped automatically—detectives may have started a 72-hour countdown to deletion once they reviewed them. It was the police, in other words, who potentially supplied that false hope.

It gets more complex. The *Guardian* didn't have to retract its claim that *NoW* had hacked Dowler's phone, because the tabloid had volunteered the information in 2002. Six days after the teen's disappearance, *NoW* approached the police with a hacked voicemail, urging investigators to follow up on a potential lead. In its own early coverage of the case, *NoW* casually referenced that message—a dead end, ultimately—with no explanation of how the tabloid had stumbled across it.

The police could have acted at any time, pursuing a case against *NoW* for its confessed hack. And in the years leading up to the furor over Dowler's missing voicemails, there were countless opportunities to target the tabloid and its parent company for hacking scores of phones. It took a false accusation—an assumption, we now know—to turn a hacking scandal into one of the biggest privacy showdowns in history.

THE POLICE COULD HAVE ACTED AT ANY TIME, PURSUING A CASE AGAINST NOW FOR ITS CONFESSED HACK.

If this sounds like a scolding, it isn't.

Privacy is too formless of a concept, and its threats too numerous, to expect a measured, rational response from the public. But the Dowler debacle exposes the ugly reality of privacy-related discourse: There is no discourse. We reel, punch-drunk, from one body blow to the next. Reports of hacks and card-skimmers and lost laptops take their toll, a wall of jabs that erodes our daily confidence. But the high-profile violations are what force us to define what privacy means, and what it's worth. When those cases involve children, all discussion tends to be drowned out. Panic is too loud, and too contagious, to be denied.

A FRESH SSN

Perhaps the central question, then, is this: Are children more vulnerable to privacy invasions than adults? The answer isn't reassuring.

In May of 2011, the "Today Show" covered a disturbing phenomenon—widespread identity theft among children. Teenagers applying for their first credit cards were discovering that their names were already attached to staggering debt ($750,000, in one case) and bankruptcies. Credit reports showed that toddlers were on the books as homeowners.

Many of these victims had their identities stolen at birth, their social security numbers guessed at by criminals. Though algorithms are used to speed up the process of trial-and-error, this is a low-tech sort of heist—social security numbers (SSNs) tend to follow specific patterns, based on the time and location they're issued. Armed sometimes with nothing but a SSN, criminals could apply for credit cards and loans, confident that few financial institutions would be willing to pay the Social Security Administration as much as $5,000 to confirm the identity associated with a given sequence (the federal agency claims that, since it discourages the use of SSNs for identification, any such cross-referencing falls outside of its regular duties). A newborn's compromised identity—or "financial birth defect," as one mother describes it—can then be used for a decade or more.

In the United States, its estimated that as many as 140,000 children per year are victims of identity theft. Compared to the roughly 8 million Americans whose identities were stolen in 2010, this might not seem like a significant statistic. But according to a 2011 study conducted by Carnegie Mellon University's CyLab, children are disproportionately targeted. The team analyzed over 800,000 records that were exposed because of data breaches, and found that while only 1 percent of the adults identities were used for fraud, 10 percent of the minors' identities were abused.

The reason for this disparity has nothing to do with predation. A SSN that has no history associated with it is less likely to raise red flags when used to open a new account, than one with 20 or 30 years of ties to someone's legitimate, recorded existence. A child's sequence is simply more versatile, and has less baggage. It's a fresh, illicit start, waiting to be used and discarded.

Preying on kids' identities, in other words, isn't necessarily the domain of perverted or particularly heinous individuals. It's good business. It's such easy money, in fact, that some parents are guilty of doing it themselves.

Linda Foley, co-founder of the Identity Theft Resource Center, recounted one such case at a conference on the topic in July 2011. The police knocked on the door of a home in Northern California, asking to speak with the resident's son. "And they insisted, so she woke him up and brought him out in his PJs. And the cops went, 'Oh.' Apparently, there was an arrest warrant out for him for failure to appear for speeding tickets, because someone had a driver's license in his name. That same person was also working using his Social Security number and name and was not paying the bills using his Social Security and his name. That person was his father."

The stories vary widely, from illegal immigrants using their children's iden-

IN THE UNITED STATES, ITS ESTIMATED THAT AS MANY AS 140,000 CHILDREN PER YEAR ARE VICTIMS OF IDENTITY THEFT.

tities to land jobs or take out credit cards, to more clear-cut abuses, such as a mother who peeled off check after bad check in her daughter's name.

So even if the Social Security Administration makes good on its promise to begin issuing numbers in random sequences, hundreds of thousands of children will remain at risk. To safeguard that most vulnerable of populations, the financial world would have to adopt an array of unique identification codes, sequences that can't simply be lifted by estranged family members or culled from data breaches.

If either of those solutions took effect, life in the United States would become that much more complex. Without the SSN as a skeleton key, the flow of personal data would slow. Loan applications might require more diligence. Users could be forced to store multiple authentication codes in secure online vaults, instead of memorizing a single nine-digit sequence. And generations of children would no longer be born potential victims.

THE 800-POUND FACEBOOK GORILLA

Unfortunately, an organized, orderly call to arms is never how privacy is restored. Despite reports from various media outlets on the apparent surge in childhood identity theft, SSN reform isn't exactly the subject of a national conversation.

Instead, all talk of kids and privacy tends to converge at a single point: Facebook. For millions of children, the world has never truly existed without it. Although the social networking giant was founded in 2004, Facebook has eclipsed its predecessors, attracting some 800 million active users, and reshaping the internet in its image. Sites across the Web now ask you to use your Facebook login, and some online services, such as the music subscription service Spotify, actually require it. Companies, bands, news organizations, nearly every person, place or thing with a Web site begs to be "Liked," a simple click of an onscreen button that broadcasts your tastes and interest to an entire network of contacts. For some, no pleading or encouragement is necessary—Likes are reflexive, and posting comments and uploading photos directly to Facebook has become a kind of muscle memory, a practiced, recurring twitch of thumbs across smartphones.

The result is an epidemic of sharing. Among teenagers, who are increasingly abandoning email and relying instead on text messages and the virtual graffiti of Facebook's wall posts, the information made semi-public is astonishing. In June 2011, a high school student in Milwaukee named Justin Cervara posted a video on Facebook, that seemed to show himself and other minors smoking marijuana. For the sake of clarity, the clip was titled "Reefer for my birthday party." Then, in late August, someone posted "I'll take five" on Cervara's wall. The 17-year-old's response, "Bro, call me ASAP," was also public. A police officer who happened to see both the video and the exchange ran across Cervara that same day, and busted him for possession.

A POLICE OFFICER WHO HAPPENED TO SEE BOTH THE VIDEO AND THE EXCHANGE RAN ACROSS CERVARA THAT SAME DAY, AND BUSTED HIM FOR POSSESSION.

This wasn't a case of the police leaning on Facebook to provide them with access to a minor's account. Cervara had surrendered his own secrets, ignoring or misreading the social networking site's privacy settings, and broadcasting his illegal actions in the clear. In other cases, teens were arrested for less dramatic, but equally ridiculous Facebook posts—including a 14-year-old boy in New Mexico who uploaded a nude photo of his 15-year-old girlfriend as revenge because she refused to sleep with him.

Police aren't the only authorities monitoring those pervasive updates. Last May, in the wake of Navy Seals killing Osama bin Laden, a 13-year-old in Tacoma, Washington, posted about his concern for retaliation against President Barack Obama. Federal authorities viewed it as a potential threat, and the boy was promptly interrogated by the Secret Service at his middle school.

Meanwhile, school districts nationwide—which are feverishly implementing and adapting anti-cyber-bullying policies—are closely monitoring the action, much to the chagrin of the ACLU and other privacy advocates. Since early 2011 alone:

■ A 13-year-old Concord, New Hampshire, girl was suspended from middle school for five days because she wrote on Facebook that she wished bin Laden had killed her math teacher instead of the 3,000 who perished on September 11, 2001.

■ A Chicago-area boy was suspended five days for creating a Facebook page dedicated to calling one of his teachers a filthy name.

■ A Lamorinda, California, student was suspended for a week, and hauled off to the police station, after posting a vague threat of violence on his page. "I would say (these types of Facebook posts are) not a regular occurrence," Associate Principal Sharon Bartlett told Miramonte High School's Mirador school newspaper. "But we see it way too often to call it rare. Since Columbine, there is no institutional sense of humor."

■ Two high school girls outside Kansas City were suspended because one made off-color remarks about the other online, leading to a fistfight at school the next day.

■ Four Stillwater High School hockey players in Minnesota were suspended for the team's rivalry game against White Bear Lake after posting an image of a teddy bear in their rivals' No. 34 jersey, with a noose around its neck. (What had presumably been simple off-color gamesmanship looked far uglier when White Bear Lake's No. 34 coincidentally suffered a season-ending knee injury during the game.)

■ A Sacramento-area high school sophomore was suspended one day for cyber-bullying, for posting on Facebook that his biology teacher was a "fat ass."

■ A high school senior in Chesapeake, Virginia, was suspended 13 days after venting frustration with a teacher who called a group report the student delivered "incoherent." The girl wrote sarcastically on Facebook that she should shoot her teacher in the face— "but then again we might not be able to carry that out since we're so incoherent."

■ A pair of seventh-graders outside Atlanta were suspended, and a third classmate was expelled, after making posts accusing a teacher of being bipolar and a pedophile. ("I was just expressing myself on Facebook," said one. "I mean, I had no intentions of ruining his reputation.")

■ A St. Petersburg, Florida, high schooler got more than she bargained for after arguing with a fellow student over a parking spot. The spat led to her car being "keyed," which led to a vague but threatening post on Facebook about bad karma for the suspected "keyer"—which led to a three-day suspension and charges of stalking from the Pinellas County Sheriff's Office.

In still other instances, it's the court of public opinion that weighs in—as in the hyper-charged national debate following the Trayvon Martin shooting, when observers attempted to analyze the teenager's character based on Facebook updates that appeared to reference marijuana. And then there are the sensitive posts, the breakups played out across the site's public walls and changes in relationship status, and the risque photos that are as visible to friends as they are to parents.

IN STILL OTHER INSTANCES, IT'S THE COURT OF PUBLIC OPINION THAT WEIGHS IN.

The obvious conclusions to be drawn are that 1) teenagers are as foolish and tone-deaf as they've always been; 2) the Internet has created a bullhorn and a written record for what had been, in previous generations, private grumbling among friends; and 3) kids don't care about No. 2; things like targeted ads are a way of life, and baring one's soul online is natural because privacy means something entirely different to the Facebook generation.

If the final point is true, that America's children have knowingly abandoned an outmoded tradition of data restriction in favor of an unbridled exchange of information, then privacy is doomed. It would mean that Facebook founder Mark Zuckerberg was right, when in early 2010 he defended the company's then-recent shift in privacy policies, which made all profiles public by default. "People have really gotten comfortable not only sharing more information and different kinds, but more openly and with more people. That social norm is just something that has evolved over time," Zuckerberg said during an interview with TechCrunch founder, Michael Arrington. If privacy wasn't already obsolete, Zuckerberg seemed intent on abolishing it. Or, at the very least, evolving past it.

ESCAPING OUR (ONLINE) PASTS

It's a compelling narrative, one that's either dystopian, utopian, or some combination of the two, depending on your perspective. A world without privacy is one without secrets, a level playing field for everyone. Or, viewed another way, it's an endless stalking ground for the criminals who subvert data wherever they can. Or maybe, according to a wide range of privacy experts, that narrative is actually nonsense. "Kids are more willing to share things, but they're sharing more of the stupid stuff," says Andrew Lewman, executive director of the Tor Project, a non-profit that distributes applications that encrypt online communications and Web browsing. "Kids have always talked to each about these things: the clothes that I have, the drinks I like. The only difference is that now, it's online."

Danah Boyd, a senior researcher at Microsoft Research who specializes in social media issues, claims that in the midst of their relentless posting, teenagers are consciously balancing the need for privacy with the benefits of publicity. During a talk at a 2010 research conference in Sweden, Boyd described an effortless sort of encryption in those posts—in-jokes that required specific knowledge to make any sense at all, song lyrics that were innocuous to some, but signaled a bout of depression to a 17-year-old's inner circle. "Privacy is of huge importance to teens because they want to have control over their lives. But publicity is also important because they want attention, support, validation, and access to broad sociality...They are entering into a social world where online performances are an essential part of social participation. Yet, they aren't engaging publicly without reservations."

> "KIDS HAVE ALWAYS TALKED TO EACH ABOUT THESE THINGS: THE CLOTHES THAT I HAVE, THE DRINKS I LIKE. THE ONLY DIFFERENCE IS THAT NOW, IT'S ONLINE."

Teenagers, of course, are endlessly influenced by how their peers view them—and when it comes to online privacy, that may be a saving grace. A November 2011 study by the Pew Research Center's Internet & American Life Project found that 55 percent of online teens had decided at one time or another not to post something online because it might reflect poorly on them in the future. One middle school girl researchers spoke with summed it up this way: "I don't want a Facebook. I'm afraid that like someday, something's going to come back and it's going to be like the end of my world because—I mean I don't know what I would do [...] But you hear stories and it just—it worries me. Like I tell all my friends who like take pictures, like, I'm like, you can't tag me in that. You can't tag anybody who's not on Facebook." This "digital withholding," as the center described it, became more prevalent with age, as 67 percent of 17 year olds surveyed said they'd reconsidered posting content with potentially negative implications.

"Kids are concerned about privacy," says Miriam Metzger, an associate professor of communication at UC Santa Barbara, whose research centers around relationships between technology, communications and our capacity to trust. "The idea that they don't care is more a myth than a reality. People, of all ages, are kind of naive in the way they interact on Facebook, not realizing that comments can be forwarded on. Things can be found later on. Crawlers can go through and pick things up."

There, again, the experts are in agreement. While it's a false assumption to imagine that kids steeped in social networking have somehow mutated into a new species, and lost their innate urge toward privacy, there are very real consequences to being lulled into oversharing. That data persists, and can be used against you in surprising ways. In 2007, a study conducted by the University of Massachusetts at Dartmouth found that nearly 20 percent of colleges and universities researched applicants on social networking sites. Those were early days, before Facebook became ubiquitous, and a boundless resource for quick and dirty background checks. By 2011, a study commissioned by Microsoft determined that 79 percent of the recruiters and hiring personnel in the United States had collected data from the internet about applicants, and that 70 percent had rejected someone based on that information. By April 2012, the practice of prospective employers demanding a job applicant's Facebook password, to more thoroughly scout for red flags, was frequent enough that lawmakers in Maryland, Illinois, California and Washington had introduced bills to outlaw it.

THOSE WERE EARLY DAYS, BEFORE FACEBOOK BECAME UBIQUITOUS, AND A BOUNDLESS RESOURCE FOR QUICK AND DIRTY BACKGROUND CHECKS.

For the Facebook generation, the problem is the quantity of information being uploaded, some of which is bound to be inadvertently damning—and often the photos that accompany it. Suddenly, it seems more likely than ever that a career or relationship-ending tidbit could resurface years later, detonating like a long-dormant, unexploded munition. It was no less than Eric Schmidt, then the CEO of Google, who told the *Wall Street Journal* in 2010, "I don't believe society understands what happens when everything is available, knowable and recorded by everyone all the time." Schmidt predicted then that the youth of American will one day be entitled to change their names upon reaching adulthood so they can distance themselves from the youthful indiscretions relentlessly catalogued online. He was being serious. "I mean we really have to think about these things as a society," he told the *Journal*. "I'm not even talking about the really terrible stuff, terrorism and access to evil things."

And, of course, whereas words on Facebook might get someone suspended, photos can have more lasting impacts. Teenagers take more pictures in high school than their parents may have captured in a lifetime, and instead of depositing them in a photo album or shoebox, these images erupt onto the internet—or onto the phones of their boyfriends and girlfriends—in a steady stream. This is an age when parents fret not only about talking with their kids about sex, but also about "sexting."

The easy explanation for the oversharing is the accessibility of the technology—cameras are cheaper, and online storage is essentially free. Alessandro Acquisti, the Associate Professor of Information Technology and Public Policy at Carnegie Mellon University, thinks there's something more nuanced at work. Our brains, Acquisti believes, can't grasp the vast stakes of uploading an image to a site that redistributes that data, copying it into multiple galleries, displaying the images to relative strangers around the globe. "In a way, we have lost that capability to understand what's private, and what's not, the way we intuitively know in a cafe, whether we should talk loudly when telling someone a

117

secret," Acquisti says. "We can see who's a friend, who's a stranger. We can gauge the risk. With social networks, that's not possible."

In one of Acquisti's ongoing experiments, when a subject is about to upload an image to Facebook, an image appears on screen. It's the face of a random person in the user's network, or it's another step removed, the face of someone in a friend's network, who's most likely a complete stranger. It's a reminder that your images, and your data, aren't being handed out to a closed circle of trusted friends and family members. It's not a whisper in a cafe, but a prolonged shout. It's an elegant way of expressing an awkward truth: Privacy has always been difficult to understand, and to defend. And it's only getting harder.

> **THE EASY EXPLANATION FOR THE OVERSHARING IS THE ACCESSIBILITY OF THE TECHNOLOGY—CAMERAS ARE CHEAPER, AND ONLINE STORAGE IS ESSENTIALLY FREE.**

THE NEXT-GEN APPROACH TO PRIVACY

What seems clear is that today's children are savvier online than they're often given credit for—but they are also growing up in a world where privacy is relentlessly compromised. The intrusions range from subtle mechanics built into social networks, to more complex surveillance from within their own families. Taser, the leading manufacturer of non-lethal weapons, is piloting a product called Defender, which lets parents follow their underage drivers progress. The GPS-enabled device plugs into the car's onboard diagnostic processor, creating a detailed, blow-by-blow log of the vehicle's whereabouts. Parents can monitor these paths online, with routes snaking across maps, calling out instances of suspected speeding, of erratic steering, acceleration or braking. If the driver veers outside of a designated area or route, Defender can release emails and text messages to their parents.

To Taser, the loss of privacy for those teenage drivers is simply part of a negotiation: You get to drive, so we, the parents, get to track your every move. Never mind that the data collected by Defender could be used against the driver in the event of an accident, or that the servers where those routes are stored could be hacked or otherwise compromised. Taser is joining a booming industry in kid surveillance, with companies already offering mirror-mounted cameras that reveal driver distraction or negligence, as well as versions of Defender's real-time tracking.

What effect will this trend have on children, already coping with a rash of so-called helicopter parenting, and now dealing with an ever-expanding data trail, tracked and logged like an ear-tagged endanger species? No one is ready to guess. Add it to the questions we have, about how big the databases will swell, what's truly happening in the Big Data industry, and how all of that resold and reused information will co-mingle in the coming years and decades.

Kids will have to decide how important the answers are, whether it justifies new laws, or some larger social and cultural reshuffling, to determine once and for all what privacy is worth. It's easy to be pessimistic, to assume that it can only get worse, and that the Facebook generation might care about privacy, but be too late to recover it.

Most of the experts we spoke to saw hope. Stanford's Ryan Calo has no doubt that privacy will be back. "It feels like we're starting to figure it out that this is important. It could be that our kids are growing up with the right values in place. They have all of the shiny new tools to protect privacy, and none of the downsides, none of the false education or assumptions of privacy that have to be unlearned," says Calo. "Maybe the next generation won't be so permissive."

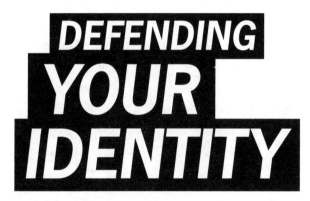

DEFENDING YOUR IDENTITY

"**W**HAT'S ON YOUR MIND?" It's the prompt that precedes every Facebook status update. And the frightening reality is, it's one key reason privacy as we know it won't last another generation.

The evolution of online journaling, from LiveJournal to MySpace to Facebook to Twitter, and whatever comes next, has created a new tradition of self-surveillance. If updates about your immediate plans and schedule aren't specific enough—"driving to work. 93's a mess, but look at these fall colors!"—Foursquare, Google Lattitude and Yelp all encourage (and sometimes reward) real-time location tracking. This is how a culture that's passed the social networking tipping point surrenders privacy—both to major corporations and the petty cybercriminals who scrape away at the underbelly of our digital infrastructure.

Over the previous eight chapters we've zoomed in on the aspects of modern life that have become vulnerable to both targeted and mass invasions of privacy. But "vulnerable" is not the same as "lost." The average citizen can take a stand, without resorting to secluded cabins in the woods or hand-written manifestos. Preventing companies from monitoring you unnecessarily, or indiscriminate hackers from rifling through your various home networks, is completely feasible. It's simply a matter of vigilance.

Defending your privacy is, in fact, much like defending against a severe storm. When severe weather warnings sound, you check to see that flashlights are stocked and loaded with working batteries. You stay alert and aware. You prepare to take more drastic action if the storm intensifies. The same approach applies to the defense of your privacy today.

The storm is here. It will find its victims. But here are ways to keep your head down until the worst of it blows over.

LOST CAUSES

Before we get into the specifics of defending privacy, it's important to note what's no longer possible. Or at least the ways in which privacy will never recover.

■ The cameras have already won. Facial recognition algorithms aren't confounded by your fake moustache. Even plastic surgery, the dramatic go-to disguise for international drug lords, only scrambles your visual data trail. It won't prevent the machines from detecting your lies, or confuse the iris scanners that are growing in popularity in law enforcement and private security circles. Your face is also probably online, out of your control, posted on Flickr and Facebook pages, with or without tags that identify you by name. There is no approval process that allows you to veto these uploads, and tags have to be actively hunted down and, where possible, deleted. Short of retiring to a mountainside someplace, your image is up for grabs, and will be populating more and more databases with each passing year.

■ Your home is being watched—not by radio-scanning hackers, but certainly by satellites, and possibly by aircraft. That funny twinge you felt the first time you used Google Maps to zoom in on your childhood backyard? That's just the beginning: In cities around the world, municipalities are enforcing building codes using aerial photography. In Riverhead, New York, residents were fined a total of $75,000 for 250 illegal swimming pools. Police can use similar flyovers to gather evidence, although they still need a search warrant to scan a house with infrared cameras. Warrantless thermal imaging was ruled unconstitutional by the U.S. Supreme Court in 2001—it had been used by police to pick out the telltale thermal glow of lamps used for marijuana production—but much of that decision was based on the uncommon nature of infrared cameras at the time. As potential snooping technology becomes commercially available, it can quickly become fair game for law enforcement. And the public records of individual homes, including their assessed value, square footage, and recent purchasing history, are freely available on websites and smartphone apps like Zillow. They're collected by Choicepoint and other data brokers, bundled together, and sold to outside buyers. If no photos are available (from a current or outdated realtor listing), Zillow will automatically import an exterior shot from Google StreetView.

■ At some point, your financial data will be compromised. The hackers are winning. Whether they're penetrating the servers of Google, the biggest data-based company in the world, or bringing down Sony's global PlayStation Network, the black hats are attacking enough major targets to eventually lay hands on virtually everyone's accounts. There are ways to limit the damage, but ultimately, the security of your money is someone else's job. Micromanaging the operations of major corporations is, from the customer's position, impossible. Luckily, most fraudulent transactions can be reversed, and most banks and credit card companies have become quite good at spotting potentially shady account activity. What's required of you is not necessarily paranoid vigilance, but awareness, and an ability to decipher your monthly statements. (Or at least to sign up for the kinds of services that sift through them for you.)

There are other lost causes, of course. There's no escaping red light cameras, no encryption technique that keeps your prescription history anonymous, and no downloadable app to block cell phone triangulation. Understanding what's lost, though, is instrumental in figuring out what's left to win—and how to fight back.

DODGE THE LOCATION LABS

Most location tracking is your own fault—in exchange for information about your surroundings, you invited a slew of different companies to track your movements. So-called location labs churn through this information and deposit it into various for-sale databases. Faked deaths and other last-ditch vanishing acts aside, here's how to broadcast less of yourself.

■ Avoid: OnStar, Electric Vehicles, and E-ZPass. The benefits of buying a car with a built-in tracking device are obvious. General Motors' OnStar service feeds vehicle telemetry data—whether the car needs servicing, when its airbags are deployed, and other sensor-based feedback—back to the company's servers. Customers are less surprised by sudden maintenance, and in the event of a serious accident, an OnStar operator can contact emergency responders on the drivers' behalf, providing real-time coordinates for the vehicle. The inevitable down side is what those services might decide to do with all that collected data—and in OnStar's case, the inevitable answer was, "Sell it." In December 2011, the service changed its privacy policy to include the line, "We may share or sell anonymized data (including location, speed, and safety belt usage) with third parties for any purpose, which may prove useful for such things as research relating to public safety or traffic services." Meanwhile, the new generation of fully electric vehicles, such as the Nissan Leaf, use a similar, persistent radio-based connection, monitoring the car's onboard battery for the first signs of a potentially explosive malfunction. There are more pedestrian uses for that datastream, though—Nissan's servers will push relevant data to the vehicle, including up-to-date locations for public chargers.

The downside of all this tracking, of course, is that you're being tracked. There's no warranty-saving way to disable these systems, the only real solution is to steer clear. The same goes for E-ZPass and similar fast-lane payment devices. The drivers in the cash-only line might be suckers, but at least there's no data trail listing the time and place of every toll they've paid in the last year or more.

■ Check: Social Network Settings. Unless you've changed your Facebook account settings, any of your "friends" can post your current location. Other services allow users to geo-tag photos, assigning precise GPS coordinates to an image of you. Dive into the settings of any site or service that includes social networking features, and restrict others from tagging you to a specific time and place. Facebook already offers location blocking, and if a company doesn't have similar options, send them emails until they do.

■ Disable: Location-Based Services. Every phone that collects your location data either asks you to approve that feature during setup, or has an option to disable it later on. In fact, most location-based smartphone apps will ask for permission every time the program is launched. Just say no, every time, in every pop-up window and menu screen there is.

There are loopholes, naturally, and one major drawback. The downside is that your highly intelligent phone is now kind of dumb.

Navigation software is revolutionary and, unless you have a fondness for atlases and asking for directions, indispensable. With a little practice, though, toggling location services on and off might be a happy middle ground. As for loopholes, at least one extremely powerful malicious app has already slipped into the Android Marketplace (*see* Chapter 4), and more are bound to find their way onto phones, with features that could very likely include location tracking. Unscrupulous apps are also likely to become more common, not quite commandeering the phone, but leeching location data without the obligatory opt-in screen. If you're reading this book, you're in luck—you aren't the blithely trusting sort, and too suspicious of free software from questionable sources.

MAINTAIN RADIO SILENCE AT HOME

Safeguarding a home from snoopers, hackers, and any combination thereof is a matter of restraint, and informed purchasing.

■ Avoid: Zigbee Devices. By the time this book hits shelves, it's possible that the device-makers who use the Zigbee wireless protocol to enable communication between appliances, sensors, and other devices throughout the home, will have employed ironclad security features to prevent signals from being spied on, or replaced with impostor commands. Pessimists might want to play it safe, and choose products that security firms approve of.

■ Check: FATS Vulnerabilities. Before setting up your own private corner of the internet of things, contact the device-makers and ask what they've done to counter possible FATS attacks, or other fingerprinting-based snooping. The solutions are simple—devices can be set to emit radio waves at random intervals, to mask when they're actually in use—but must be implemented at the design stage.

■ Isolate: Embedded Devices. Remember that demonstration that showed how internet-connected TVs can be hijacked, allowing hackers to insert false pages into big-screen web browsing, or collect your login information for paid services (such as Netflix) accessed directly by the display? If that sort of net-accessing feature is why you bought the TV, you can choose to do nothing and hope for the best (the odds are clearly in your favor). If, like so many features buried in embedded devices, dipping your flatscreen into the murky, malicious waters of the internet isn't essential to your viewing experience, turn off the connection. Limit financial info to the machines and environments that have dedicated security measures—computers protected by software, or mobile applications from developers you trust.

FOCUS ON YOUR PHONE

As discussed earlier, the very things that make a smartphone "smart" are at the same functions that pose a threat to their users' privacy. You could, of course, forego the modern convenience of the devices and stick with that trusty flip phone that's been doing yeoman's work for a decade. But if you like having technological wizardry at your fingertips that would have struck our forefathers as no less than utter black magic, here are ways to protect yourself.

■ Avoid: Android Phones. At the risk of taking sides in the battle between Apple's operating system, iOS, and Google's Android platform, the search giant's open-source approach to smartphones is a security disaster waiting to happen. While Apple has developed a thorough (and, at times, inscrutable) approval process for submissions to its App Store, the Android Marketplace is free-spirited pioneer territory, with well-intentioned freeware rubbing shoulders with the occasional digital snake oil. Android has the benefit of allowing developers to create security software for it. Unfortunately, hackers have already demonstrated the ability to insert malicious code deep into the operating system, deeper than any security app can currently function. Apple's own store hasn't been immune to shady apps, but none have compromised iOS itself. And as Android continues to outpace iOS for overall cellphone marketshare, it's simply more efficient to focus attacks on the bigger operating system. Whether they're in it for cash, or bragging rights, Android offers hackers more bang for their bugs.

■ Acknowledge: Apple's not perfect, either. In February 2012, the company came under fire when researchers discovered that some apps were siphoning off users' address book information without their knowledge. Turns out, that wasn't all. Starting with the release of iOS4 in 2010, Apple inserted a more disquieting loophole into the user agreements: When owners allowed apps on their mobile devices to access their location information, the app was also given permission to copy the user's entire photo library, without any further notification or warning. That's compounded by the fact that when i-device owners take photos and record videos, GPS coordinates of the photo spot are generally embedded in the files, creating quite a clear visual and geographic trail. And what an app designer might do with that information once they've pulled it off a device is completely out of Apple's control.

More flashy—and potentially fishy—iPhone technology came to light in May 2012, when the chief information officer at IBM, Jeanette Horan, told MIT's Technology Review about some of IBM's security protocols for employees' mobile devices. Among them? Immediately banning Siri, the iPhone's voice-activated digital assistant, which can dictate text messages and emails, launch Web searches, and which had become enough of a breakout star to be featured alongside famous actors in Apple's commercials. It turns out, according to Apple's iOS5 software license agreement, everything users say to Siri is recorded and sent back to an Apple data center to be converted into text. Furthermore, "Your device will also send Apple other information, such as your first name and nickname; the names, nicknames, and relationship with you (e.g., 'my dad') of your address book contacts; and song names in your collection (collectively, your 'User Data'). All of this data is used to help Siri and Dictation understand you better and recognize what you say." Horan didn't want to risk proprietary information accidentally ending up on Apple's servers. "We're just extraordinarily conservative," she told the journal. "It's the nature of our business."

■ Check: Password-Protect Your Mobile Devices. A recent study commissioned by Symantec underscored a disheartening reality: Losing your smartphone is liable to cost more than just a new piece of hardware. After deliberately leaving 50 smartphones in New York City, Los Angeles, Washington D.C., San Francisco and Ottawa, Canada, Symantec's "Honey Stick Project" showed that finders made an effort to return the devices only half the time. But virtually every finder—96 percent of them—tried to access the device, and there was an 89 percent chance the finder looked for personal information on it. (Sixty percent of the finders tried to view photos and email accounts linked there, and eighty percent tried to dig through corporate files with names like "HR Salaries," which Symantec had preloaded on to the devices. Half the finders even tried to access a bank account linked to the phone.) "Just giving the phone password-based security would have prevented the casual finder from trolling through the data," writes Kevin Haley, who spearheaded the project for Symantec. The security guru also advocates for the use of software that can locate your lost phone—and even remotely lock or wipe it should it go missing.

KEEP HEALTH RECORDS CONFIDENTIAL

Although you have no control over how hospitals, insurance providers, pharmacies and doctors handle your health data, a few simple choices will reduce your exposure.

■ Avoid: Snip Sequencing. The threat of data reuse should be clear by now. When that data reveals your genetic predisposition towards specific diseases or conditions, as well as hints at what syndromes your parents may have, or what your children could develop, the potential privacy violation looms over entire families. So while companies like 23andMe can sequence a limited "snip" of your DNA, and provide fascinating guesses at where your ancestors were born, and how you might die, there's a real risk that your genetic fragment will be sold to a third party. Even if present-day policies only allow for reuse with your permission, databases are immortal. The safest bet isn't to trust that sequencing operations will keep their word, and resist selling off bundles of decoded snips for easy money. Snip sequencing puts your DNA in the hands of people who don't have medical licenses to lose, and have everything to gain from reuse.

■ Check: Your Pharmacy's Privacy Policy. Don't bother looking for answers online or in the obtuse documentation that comes attached to your prescriptions—call your pharmacy, and ask what they do with your prescription history. Is that information shared with any partner companies? Does their policy allow them to sell that data to third parties, and what sort of notification is issued to customers if and when those privacy rules change?

Chances are, you will be treated like a crazy person. That doesn't matter. These are questions that any business should answer, and there is indisputable evidence that prescription histories are for sale, and have been for years. Expect larger drugstore chains to bounce you throughout their corporate communications staff. And if answers aren't forthcoming, or what you were hoping for, expect to deal with the possible hassle of abandoning the megalithic pharmacies altogether. Smaller pharmacies may take longer to fill some prescriptions, but with a fraction of the customer base, they have less to offer, and less to gain by betraying your privacy.

In case anyone assures you that your history is shared, but ano-nymized—that your name is replaced by a series of numbers or other characters—remember all of the studies, academic papers, and court documents that have demonstrated how easy re-identification is. Don't explain any of that. Take your data and run.

LOOK BEFORE YOU TYPE (AND SWIPE)

Once your financial digits—your credit card numbers, your bank account number, and any associated security codes—enter another system, you are powerless to protect them. That burden falls to Bank of America, and the mom-and-pop hardware store, and everyone you do business with, whether online or in person. For those not ready to resort to a truly paranoid, cash-only lifestyle, your responsibility is to be observant, and resist handing your financial life over to impostors.

■ Avoid: Debit Card Purchases. If the worst happens, and your numbers are lifted—fed into a false Web site, hoovered up by a check-out line "skimmer," or read over the phone to a fake or felonious sales rep—the damage is rarely irrevocable. Reversing charges or transfers from a bank account, however, is harder than convincing your credit card company that you've been victimized. Credit card providers are battle-hardened victims themselves, with decades of experience recovering from millions in annual losses. They also employ advanced, artificial intelligence-backed fraud detection algorithms that can spot bogus charges before you do. Banks, on the other hand, are willing to hand over bags of money to anyone with an ominous note. That's not to say you should shred your debit cards. But limit their use, particularly for online shopping or payments.

■ Check: Every Transaction Page, Every ATM. There are no hard-and-fast rules for spotting a phishing site. The poorly executed versions are obvious. Suddenly, the URL address doesn't read BestBuy.com, but a scramble of gibberish, ending with a ".za" or ".de," indicating that whatever page you're on hails from servers in a foreign country. Or logos vanish, and the website's text becomes riddled with typos. Experienced phishers, however, are true counterfeiters, closely mirroring the layout, language, and URLs of the sites they've siphoned you away from.

The proper response is to be unreasonably suspicious. Look for "https" in the address bar, indicating a secure payment server, which requires a paper trail that phishers rarely want to risk creating. If anything seems out of place, or uncharacteristically sloppy, call customer support. The same goes for emails asking you to confirm your account info. The wording might be official, but oddly phrased, and probably doesn't matter— institutions don't pester their customers with random emails to confirm their passwords. If there's any doubt, again, call customer support.

This is important, though: Never call any of the phone numbers listed on a "phishy" webpage or email. Open a new browser window, navigate a new path to the site or company's contact info, and go from there.

The physical analog to phishing is skimming, and although no one should expect to spot a subtle change in the card swiping interface at the register of the local arts and crafts store, the false fronts attached to ATMs are easier to catch. Still, these aren't slap-dash illusions—they're masks, glued over the original card slot, and designed to be removed in short order. Look for uneven seams, an odd, protruding sense of bulk, a general DIY aesthetic that doesn't exactly scream "bank."

■ Encrypt: Account Numbers. This last ditch tactic is inconvenient, time-consuming, and somewhat brilliant. Most card providers allow their customers to create single-use, disposable stand-ins for their account numbers. The logistics are aggravating—once you've decided what you're paying for, you have to sign into your credit card account online (usually through a secure program that you've downloaded and installed ahead of time), generate the code, and then switch back to the original payment screen to paste it into the correct field. The result, however, is an unbreakable act of encryption. Whether the site you've purchased from is real or a ruse, the owner has never seen your actual card number, much less squirreled it away. Of course, this trick makes it impossible to save your card info, or to set up automatic or scheduled payments. Until recently, this feature was unique to Discover, but now all of the major card providers offer similar self-destructing payment codes. And even if you aren't ready to encrypt every online transaction, it's a relatively easy way to alleviate any doubts about lesser known shopping sites.

JOINING THE CYBERWAR

The war on privacy is a roiling, global conflict, fought in the courts, in the halls of Congress, and in the marketplace—the products you buy to protect yourself, and the products that criminals reverse-engineer and exploit. The frontlines, though, are where there's the most to gain, and everything to lose. The internet teems with malicious code, waiting in ambush on the other side of false links, latched onto innocent or urgent-sounding email, and taking root deep in the operating systems of millions of computers. Fighting back isn't optional. Anyone with internet access has already been drafted.

■ Basic Training. Many computer intrusions will shatter against standard security software. So-called firewalls, which allow essentially any outgoing data to pass, but attempt to verify all incoming code, are a given in modern networking gear and anti-virus programs. Office-based networks will often restrict or deflect more data than the average home-based setup, but in both cases, there's nothing much for you (assuming you're not in the IT department) to fiddle with. Anti-virus software adds another layer of defense, recognizing the more cleverly disguised programs based on regular updates of known threats—the rough, digital equivalent of receiving and memorizing a daily pile of most-wanted posters. Most of these unsavory programs are picked up after they've nested in the computer or phone's memory. If firewalls are a walled perimeter with an armed checkpoint, anti-virus software is your police force, patrolling the streets for troublemakers.

Picking a specific software suite is a personal choice—McAfee, Kaspersky and Symantec all make a concerted effort to stay on top of the evolving threats, and all offer a variety of prices for monthly or annual coverage. Macintosh users, in general, can stick with Apple's own security updates. Apple computers aren't immune to viruses—as the "Flashback" trojan earlier this year demonstrated—but with a market share still in the single digits, they aren't the target of opportunity that Windows machines appear to be.

■ Counter: Spyware. Although nearly all malicious software can be gathered under the umbrella of malware, spyware deserves special attention. This is code that is often more subtle than a true virus or worm, downloading onto the computer as part of the normal webpage loading process, and gradually exerting control. The effects can vary, from forcing the user to the same webpage every time the browser launches, to replacing the desktop background with a company's logo and promotional material, offering security software that, believe it or not, will block incoming malware. More insidious, maybe, is the spyware that grinds away in secret, reporting your web activity to a third party.

Traditional security software can eliminate a good deal of spyware, but dedicated spy-hunting programs are better. Both Adaware and Spybot S&D (short for search and destroy) are free to download and use, with the option to purchase additional protection later.

■ Avoid: Scareware. In a trend that's as cunning as it is cruel, users are being baited with offers of free security software, or updates of existing security software. Called "scareware" because they tend to make contact as an alarming email or pop-up alert, these programs are usually constitute a new phishing technique, requiring you to enter personal information to confirm the download and installation. According to Microsoft, there were 4 million scareware infections in the second quarter of 2010, many of which involved programs that looked like Microsoft products, taking advantage of the company's own busy download schedule of security updates. Avoiding this scam is a matter of familiarizing yourself with your security software's interface, never clicking on a security update prompt that appears in your web browser, and researching any free security software before inviting it inside.

■ Check: Glitchy Hardware. If and when a nasty string of code slips through your best defenses and browsing practices, there are symptoms of infection to be aware of. A machine that's suddenly sluggish to turn on, that stalls when launching programs, or is generally slower than usual while online, might be host to any number of unwanted applications. Malware can fill free storage memory with propagating code, or, in the case of a botnet infection, clog your internet connection with mass spam messages and attempts to spread its zombie-like pathogen. Other hardware problems can indicate the worst possible intrusion: a direct, remote takeover of the computer or its components. In 2008, a Florida woman noticed that her computer's battery was draining faster than normal, and the light next to the embedded webcam seemed to blink at random. She turned out to be one of nine women who were being watched, and photographed, by a hacker who had planted malicious software while servicing their computers. Bizarre computer performance merits a close inspection of your installed applications, and possibly a trip to a computer repair shop.

■ Encrypt: Email Addresses. After years of embarrassing security breaches of Windows, Internet Explorer, and its online email service, Hotmail, Microsoft has of late been winning praise from privacy advocates.

One interesting feature is the ability to create up to five email aliases in Hotmail. Like the single-use account numbers offered by credit card companies, these aliases shield your real email address from being sucked into spam databases, and sold to third parties or reused for tracking purposes. Incoming messages to a given alias can be filtered into separate folders, or cut off entirely. It also means that personally identifying characters in an email address—part or all of your name, for example—can remain private.

■ Check: Email Password Strength. Use a secure password checker to guarantee your super secret letter-and-number combination is as robust as possible. Microsoft, for instance, has a webpage devoted to analyzing the strength of hypothetical passwords. Is this bullet point rudimentary? Yes. But the most embarrassing of breaches can happen in the simplest of ways: In October 2011, a 35-year-old Florida man was arrested and charged with hacking the email accounts of dozens of female celebrities, then spreading the intimate photos he found there across the web. He'd guessed the celebrities' passwords by nothing more than monitoring tabloids and social media accounts for clues like a favorite author or a pet's name.

■ Disrupt: Online Tracking. The previous tips should secure your computer, and your online activity, from the worst of the security threats. Now, let's deal with the murkier privacy threat of our times: the strange, seedy business of online tracking. Most of the information collected by Big Data is through spying—not though spyware, but so-called cookies, snippets of code that allow your browser to remember which sites you've visited, speeding up the loading process when you return. Unfortunately, cookies tend to have their own agenda, and can report back to various entities about your web-based wandering. That data is harvested to create a profile of who you appear to be—which is then sold and resold throughout different industries.

The first step to dismantling those tracking profiles is to replace the bad cookies with better ones. The major online advertiser networks offer so called opt-out cookies, which will prevent their own cookies from latching on to your browser. They should also prevent the network and its partners from serving you behavioral advertising—the ads that appear to know what you're searching for, and what you're discussing in email, spitting out listings of funeral homes when you make an overly morbid joke, or discounts on diabetes-related supplies as you read up on the disease.

Don't waste your time rifling through ad network sites to gather opt-out cookies. Services like PrivacyChoice centralize the process, allowing you to opt-out of all of them at once. PrivacyChoice includes additional tools that let you clear your current profiles, and show, in real-time, which companies are tracking the sites that you visit.

Microsoft's latest version of its Internet Explorer (IE) browser goes one step further. The Tracking Protection feature is designed to deflect all tracking cookies, as well as the more subtle scripts that collect data on the spot, or trigger behavioral ads. It took Microsoft some time to work out the kinks, but with the full release of IE9, the feature is simple and robust, and an example that other browser-makers might be forced to follow.

We covered the Do Not Track (DNT) header in Chapter 5, but as of this writing, the only company to adopt this concept is Mozilla, the makers of the Firefox browser. When activated, the header embeds a clear, unmistakable demand to every site the user visits: do not track me...or else. It's the "or else" part of that's still in flux. By the time you read this, it's possible that the FTC will have enacted industry-wide restrictions on tracking, with the DNT header as the central method for keeping the advertising networks in line (providing they're forced to comply with it). Or, in an ironic twist, it could be used as an enforcement tool, with volunteers allowing the creators of the DNT header to monitor their own activity, with a cookie-like script that reports back on which sites and companies are ignoring the header. If nothing else moves forward, Firefox users can at least activate the DNT header, and hope that the trackers get the message.

■ **Encrypt: All Online Activity.** The last word in online privacy is Tor. It stands for The Onion Router, referring to an encryption technique that transmits data through multiple layers of connections. Instead of an email traveling in a relatively straight line, with associated data markers showing how and when it was sent, Tor bounces the email throughout the world, between volunteer host networks, before it lands, free of any useful information about its point of origin. The same goes for browsing, as Tor's global relay system scrambles any attempts to track the user. Companies can still build profiles of Tor users who visit a given site, but that profile won't include the normal range of data—what country, state, city and county the user is accessing the internet from, what his or her computer specifications are, what site or service sent them to the site, and any name or identity. Tor users are apparitions, blinking in and out of existence.

Tor is a spy game, essentially. It turns everyday browsing into a covert operation. That's also it's biggest drawback. Browsing through Tor—which can be used in a number of ways, but the easiest is through a free, downloadable Firefox add-on—blocks cookies indiscriminately, making the shopping carts on sites like Amazon relatively useless. It also frequently boots you from sites and services that require some sort of cookie to confirm your identity during regular navigation. So nearly all Tor users also browse unprotected, toggling back and forth depending on their activity. The moment that browsing activity overlaps, the apparition becomes solid. If you happen to go to CNN.com from your Tor-protected browser window, and then accidentally head back to that site during the same session, from your standard browser window, CNN and its tracking partners will be able to synchronize the two visitors into a single profile. Tor requires dilligence, and patience—it's notoriously slow, with all those fast-passes through scattered routers sometimes resulting in load times last seen in the dial-up era.

Yet Tor represents something bigger. The Tor Foundation claims that downloads have skyrocketed in recent years, and that its user base has gone from highly tech-savvy to completely mainstream.

NAVIGATING SOCIAL NETWORKS

The more ubiquitous Facebook, and its competitors, become, the more they reach deeper into our lives. And what they can expose should be guarded with the strictest of diligence.

■ Check: Facebook Settings (Again). Tracking companies are using Facebook more and more to beef up their profiles. Some of this happens through various friending gimmicks, or marketing-related efforts to get people to "like" specific groups or corporate Facebook profiles. The data collection goes much deeper than that, however. Facebook applications, which inherently require you to share your information, can share that data with entities completely removed from the service. The end-results can be startling. If you've installed the Flixster Facebook application, and happen to visit the movie site RottenTomatoes.com, your profile photo, along with a selection of your friends, will pop into view. Other partnerships are less obvious, with no clear indicators that cross-platform tracking is occurring.

One response is to clean out Facebook applications that you no longer use. The next level is to dump all of the applications, and to dig into the service's privacy features and restrict as much as you can. This won't guarantee that your Facebook profile will be off-limits, particularly to the social networking viruses that security analysts claim are inevitable.

■ Safeguard: Your Password. To restate the obvious: Do not give anyone else control of your page, including spouses or potential employers who ask for it during job interviews. In fact, it's part the Rights and Responsibilities Facebook users agree to: "You will not share your password ... (or) let anyone else access your account." It's more important now than ever, as "Social forensics," as recruiters are calling it, becomes more common in both HR departments and living rooms across the country. And it's not helping in either place.

In one workplace incident that made national news, a 27-year-old elementary school teacher's aide in Michigan named Kimberly Hester was called before her superintendent because of a potentially lewd photo a student's parent had seen on Hester's Facebook page. The superintendent demanded access to her page. The picture, sent as a joke by another teacher and viewable only to the aide's friends, showed the subject's shoes, with their pants down around their ankles. Hester refused to hand over her password; a letter from the district soon followed: "In the absence of you voluntarily granting Lewis Cass ISD administration access to you[r] Facebook page," it read, "we will assume the worst and act accordingly." Hester was ultimately fired—and is now embroiled in a legal battle with the district over what she says was unlawful termination.

Meanwhile, thanks to a 2009 study by psychology professors at the University of Guelph in Ontario, Canada, "Facebook jealousy" is now an established—and destructive—phenomenon in romantic relationships. Researchers found that a combination of inappropriate flirtatiousness and friends reporting questionable behavior to a spouse can create a toxic feedback loop for couples. "Our study provides evidence of Facebook's unique contributions to the experience of jealousy in romantic relationships," the authors wrote—and it's having tangible effects: In 2011, a study by a divorce firm in the United Kingdom found that 33 percent of behavior complaints in its filings involved the word "Facebook."

With social networking's potential downsides, for every age group, one instinct might be to abandon your account entirely. But assuming you still want access to the party invitations and your nephew's baby photos, the smarter option is simply to scrub your profile entirely, turning it into a blank, white slate, and ensuring that no one will be able to access or data-mine long after you've logged off.

In more than a century since Samuel Warren and Louis Brandeis first weighed in on the right to privacy in the Harvard Law Review, the priorities and technologies have evolved in ways they scarcely could have imagined. Today, opportunities abound for mass privacy invasions at the hands of a government claiming a war on terror, software companies claiming they've built the killer app, and scammers just updating ancient ways to make a cheap buck. Together, they can—and will—make targets of anyone. Yet, there's some counterintuitive comfort there: The bigger and more careless the herd, the less likely informed citizens are to be targeted by predators. Those who remain attentive can slip beneath the rising tide of pointlessly revealing status updates and unsecured transactions. The storm is upon us. But you can be prepared. No one said privacy had to die quietly.

EXPERTS CONSULTED

CHAPTER ONE: YOU
Ryan Calo, Research Director for privacy and robotics, Stanford University's Center for Internet and Society
Beth Givens, Director, Privacy Rights Clearinghouse

CHAPTER TWO: YOUR LOCATION
Beth Givens, Director, Privacy Rights Clearinghouse
Jim Harper, Director of Information Policy Studies, Cato Institute
Jonathan McPhie, Privacy lead for Google+, project manager, Google
Lee Tien, Senior Staff Attorney, EFF

CHAPTER THREE: YOUR HOME
Adrian Turner, CEO, Mocana

CHAPTER FOUR: YOUR PHONE
Susan Landau, Visiting Scholar in the department of Computer Science, Harvard University
Roel Schouwenberg, Senior Malware Researcher, Kasperksy Labs

CHAPTER FIVE: YOUR COMPUTER
Jim Brock, CEO/Founder, PrivacyChoice
Jonathan Mayer, Graduate Student, Stanford University
Jonathan McPhie, Privacy lead for Google+, project manager, Google
Arvind Naranayan, post-doctoral computer science researcher, Stanford University
Ashkan Soltani, privacy and security consultant and researcher
Sid Stamm, Lead Privacy Engineer, Mozilla

CHAPTER SIX: YOUR MONEY
Roel Schouwenberg, Senior Malware Researcher, Kasperksy Labs

CHAPTER SEVEN: YOUR DNA

Jim Brock, CEO/Founder, Privacy Choice
Ryan Calo, Research Director for privacy and robotics,
  Stanford University Center for Internet and Society
Jeremy Gruber, President and Executive Director,
  Council for Responsible Genetics
Deven McGraw, Director of the Health Privacy Project,
  Center for Democracy and Technology
Lee Tien, Senior Staff Attorney, EFF

CHAPTER EIGHT: YOUR KIDS

Alessandro Acquisti, Associate Professor of information technology and
  public policy, Carnegie Mellon University's CyLab
Danah Boyd, Senior Researcher, Microsoft Research
Andrew Lewman, Executive Director, Tor Foundation
Miriam Metzger, Associate Professor of Communication, UC Santa Barbara

CHAPTER NINE: DEFENDING YOUR IDENTITY

This chapter draws on research and interviews related to the rest of the book.
  Of great help:
Jim Brock, CEO/Founder, Privacy Choice
Andrew Lewman, Executive Director, Tor Foundation

NOTES

CHAPTER 1: YOU

"The Right to Privacy"; Harvard Law Review (groups.csail.mit.edu), December 15, 1890.
http://groups.csail.mit.edu/mac/classes/6.805/articles/privacy/Privacy_brand_warr2.html

"Surveillance Society: New High-Tech Cameras Are Watching You"; popularmechanics.com, October 2009.
www.popularmechanics.com/technology/military/4236865

"Surveillance Cameras in Public Places—CCTV Video Surveillance to Combat Terrorism," popularmechanics.com, May 2010.
www.popularmechanics.com/technology/how-to/computer-security/surveillance-cameras-and-data

"The Future of Surveillance—When Automated Brains Keep Watch 24/7"; popularmechanics.com, May 26, 2010.
www.popularmechanics.com/technology/how-to/computer-security/future-of-surveillance-cameras

"AAAS 4: Surveillance—The Good, The Bad, And The Questionable"; popularmechanics.com, October 1, 2009.
www.popularmechanics.com/science/2336481

"FBI's Next-Gen ID Databank to Store Face Scans—A Good Idea?"; popularmechanics.com, June 30, 2008.
www.popularmechanics.com/science/health/forensics/4270770

"Brockton Experiment with Facial Recognition Technology Raises Civil Liberties Concerns"; aclum.org, June 22, 2010.
www.aclum.org/news_6.22.10

"Automated Face Analysis"; cs.cmu.edu.
www.cs.cmu.edu/afs/cs/project/face/www/Facial.htm

"Avatar Border Agent Knows When You're Lying"; inhardfocus.com, March 1, 2011.
http://inhardfocus.com/inhardfocus/tag/lie-detector

"AVATAR Kiosk: Interactive screening technology"; chatbots.org, March 8, 2011.
www.chatbots.org/conversational/agent/avatar_virtual_agent_biometrics

"East Coast Grocery Chain uses Facial Recognition Surveillance";
securityworldnews.com, March 18, 2010.
www.securityworldnews.com/2010/03/18/east-coast-grocery-chain-uses-facial-recognition-surveillance

"FaceEXPLORER: Face recognition to identify known criminals"; l1id.com.
www.l1id.com/pages/78-faceexplorer

"Next Generation Identification"; fbi.gov.
www.fbi.gov/about-us/cjis/fingerprints_biometrics/ngi/ngi2

"New Orleans Scrapping Surveillance Cameras"; schneier.com, October 28, 2010.
www.schneier.com/blog/archives/2010/10/new_orleans_scr.html

Privacy in Peril: How We Are Sacrificing a Fundamental Right in Exchange for Security and Convenience. James B. Rule. Oxford University Press, 2009. 978-0195394368

Schneier on Security. Bruce Schneier. Wiley, 2008. 978-0470395356

"Facial Recognition Technology, A Survey of Policy and Implementation Issues";
The Center for Catastrophe Preparedness and Response (nyu.edu/ccpr).
www.nyu.edu/ccpr/pubs/Niss_04.08.09.pdf

"Faces of Facebook: Privacy in the Age of Augmented Reality";
Carnegie Mellon University.
www.heinz.cmu.edu/~acquisti/face-recognition-study-FAQ

"Face-off over Super Bowl spying"; securityfocus.com, March 9, 2003.
www.securityfocus.com/news/170

CHAPTER 2: YOUR LOCATION

"6 Mods for the Ultimate High-Tech Police Car"; popularmechanics.com,
July 22, 2009.
www.popularmechanics.com/cars/news/industry/4325540

"Law Enforcement Use of Global Positioning (GPS) Devices to Monitor Motor
Vehicles: Fourth Amendment Considerations"; Congressional Research
Service (fas.org), February 28, 2011.
www.fas.org/sgp/crs/misc/R41663.pdf

"City Cops' Plate Scanner is a License to Snoop"; schneier.com, September 19, 2004.
www.schneier.com/essay-057.html

NOTES

"Location and Privacy: Where are we headed on Data Privacy Day?";
technet.com, January 26, 2011.
http://blogs.technet.com/b/microsoft_on_the_issues/archive/2011/01/26/
location-and-privacy-where-are-we-headed-on-data-privacy-day-natu-
ral-user-interface.aspx

"Investigations of Google Street View"; epic.org.
http://epic.org/privacy/streetview

"E-ZPass records make way into criminal and civil trials"; Baltimore Sun,
September 2, 2007.
www.boston.com/news/nation/articles/2007/09/02/e_zpass_records_
make_way_into_criminal_and_civil_trials

"Inspector General's Probe Prompts Conviction at Manhattan Psychiatric Center
(E-ZPass Records Exposed Overtime Scam)"; New York State Inspector
General (readmedia.com), September 23, 2009.
http://readme.readmedia.com/Inspector-Generals-Probe-Prompts-Con-
viction-at-Manhattan-Psychiatric-Center/956348

"30 NYPD Narcotics Officers Are Shifted in Shake-Up Linked to Overtime";
The New York Times, November 17, 2003.
www.policeone.com/news/72286-30-NYPD-Narcotics-Officers-Are-
Shifted-in-Shake-Up-Linked-to-Overtime

"E-ZPass Ticket To Divorce Court"; bauerfamilylaw.blogspot.com, August 11, 2007.
http://bauerfamilylaw.blogspot.com/2007/08/e-zpass-ticket-to-divorce-court.html

"Toll records catch unfaithful spouses'" usatoday.com, August 10, 2007.
www.usatoday.com/tech/news/surveillance/2007-08-10-ezpass_N.htm

"Man who killed 5 kids called strict, controlling, jealous"; seattlepi.com,
April 5, 2009.
www.seattlepi.com/local/article/Man-who-killed-5-kids-called-strict-
controlling-1303164.php

US Court of Appeals Ruling vs. Juan Pineda-Moreno; August 12, 2010.
www.ca9.uscourts.gov/datastore/opinions/2010/08/12/08-30385.pdf

"Canadian man pleads guilty to April Oak Brook murder (Dmitry Smirnov
admits stalking, luring and killing woman he met online in 2008)";
chicagotribune.com, July 22, 2011.
http://articles.chicagotribune.com/2011-07-22/news/chi-canadian-man-pleads-guilty-
to-april-westmont-murder-20110722_1_canadian-man-jitka-vesel-dmitry-smirnov

147

2222222222
222
2222
222222

"Privacy Invasion Curtailed"; nytimes.com, February 13, 2003.
www.nytimes.com/2003/02/13/opinion/privacy-invasion-curtailed.html

The Googlization of Everything And Why We Should Worry.
Siva Vaidhyanathan. University of California Press, 2011. 978-0520258822

The Watchers: The Rise of America's Surveillance State. Shane Harris.
Penguin Press, 2010. 978-1594202452

"iPhone Tracker"; Alasdair Allan and Pete Warden.
http://petewarden.github.com/iPhoneTracker/#faq

"Congressmen query Apple on changes to privacy policy"; CNET.com, June 24, 2010.
http://news.cnet.com/8301-31021_3-20008721-260.html

"Apple, Google Collect User Data"; wsj.com, April 21, 2011.
http://online.wsj.com/article/SB10001424052748703983704576277101723453610.html

CHAPTER 3: YOUR HOME
"Gadgets Get the Internet"; connectedworldmag.com, March 9, 2011.
www.connectedworldmag.com/latestNewsaspx?id=NEWS110308151745567

"Protecting your Daily In-Home Activity Information from a Wireless
Snooping Attack"; University of Virgnia.
www.cs.virginia.edu/~whitehouse/research/fats/srinivasan08protecting.pdf

"SmartGrid Device Security — Adventures in a new medium"; Black Hat USA 2009.
www.blackhat.com/presentations/bh-usa-09/MDAVIS/BHUSA09-Davis-AMI-SLIDES.pdf

"The Friendly Traitor: Our Software Wants to Kill Us"; inguardians.com.
http://inguardians.com/pubs/FriendlyTraitor.pdf

"Hacking the Smart Grid"; technologyreview.com, April 5, 2010.
www.technologyreview.com/news/418320/hacking-the-smart-grid

"PlayStation Network hackers access data of 77 million users"; guardian.co.uk,
April 26, 2011.
www.guardian.co.uk/technology/2011/apr/26/playstation-network-hackers-data

"Sony PlayStation suffers massive data breach"; reuters.com, April 26, 2011.
www.reuters.com/article/2011/04/26/us-sony-stoldendata-idUS-TRE73P6WB20110426

NOTES

"Sony faces legal action over attack on PlayStation network"; bbc.com,
April 28, 2011.
www.bbc.com/news/technology-13192359

"California Man Pleads Guilty in 'Botnet' Attack That Impacted Seattle
Hospital and Defense Department"; justice.gov, May 4, 2006.
www.justice.gov/criminal/cybercrime/press-releases/2006/maxwellPlea.htm

"'Botnet' hacker sentenced to 3 years"; seattletimes.nwsource.com, August 26, 2006.
http://seattletimes.nwsource.com/html/localnews/2003226994_botnet26m.html

CHAPTER 4: YOUR PHONE
"How Vegas Security Drives Surveillance Tech Everywhere";
popularmechanics.com, January 1, 2010.
www.popularmechanics.com/technology/how-to/computer-security/4341499

"Hacker Spoofs Cell Phone Tower to Intercept Calls"; wired.com, July 31, 2010.
www.wired.com/threatlevel/2010/07/intercepting-cell-phone-calls

"Olmstead v. United States"; Supreme Court of the United States
(law.cornell.edu), June 4, 1928.
www.law.cornell.edu/supct/html/historics/USSC_CR_0277_0438_ZS.html

"Tice: NSA mixed spying with credit card data"; zdnet.com, January 23, 2009.
www.zdnet.com/blog/government/tice-nsa-mixed-spying-with-credit-card-data/4296

"The Fed Who Blew the Whistle"; thedailybeast.com, December 12, 2008.
www.thedailybeast.com/newsweek/2008/12/12/the-fed-who-blew-the-whistle.html

"The Federal Government and My Privacy"; pbs.org, May 15, 2007.
www.pbs.org/wgbh/pages/frontline/homefront/preemption/privacy.html

"Examining the recent Android malware"; iss.net; March 3, 2011.
http://blogs.iss.net/archive/Examining%20the%20recent.html

"Why gadget makers wield a "kill switch""; cnn.com, May 12, 2011.
www.cnn.com/2011/TECH/mobile/05/12/kill.switch/index.html?hpt=C2

"The Athens Affair—How some extremely smart hackers pulled off the most
audacious cell-network break-in ever"; spectrum.ieee.org, July 2007.
http://spectrum.ieee.org/telecom/security/the-athens-affair

The Watchers: The Rise of America's Surveillance State. Shane Harris. Penguin Press, 2010. 978-1594202452

"Lawful Electronic Surveillance in the Face of New Technologies — Testimony of Susan Landau"; Joint Hearing of the Technology and Law Senate subcommittee, February 17, 2011.
http://judiciary.house.gov/hearings/pdf/Landau02172011.pdf

"Android Security Test"; androidsecuritytest.com.
http://androidsecuritytest.com/features/logs-and-services/loggers/carrieriq

"Carrier IQ Tries to Censor Research With Baseless Legal Threat"; eff.org, November 21, 2011.
www.eff.org/deeplinks/2011/11/carrieriq-censor-research-baseless-legal-threat

"Carrier IQ, HTC, Samsung Sued Over Tracking Software"; talkingpointsmemo.com, December 2, 2011.
http://idealab.talkingpointsmemo.com/2011/12/carrier-iq-htc-samsung-sued-over-tracking-software.php

"Results of Nationwide Government Cell Phone Tracking Records Request Show Frequent Violations of Americans' Privacy Rights"; aclu.org, March 31, 2012.
www.aclu.org/blog/technology-and-liberty-national-security/results-nationwide-government-cell-phone-tracking

CHAPTER 5: YOUR COMPUTER

"California Senate OKs Gmail Bill, Drops Marketing Restrictions"; dmnews.com, June 1, 2004.
www.dmnews.com/california-senate-oks-gmail-bill-drops-marketing-restrictions/article/84348

"Calif. Senate OKs Email Scanning Limits"; crn.com, May 28, 2004.
www.crn.com/news/channel-programs/18842909/calif-senate-oks-email-scanning-limits.htm

"Privacy leakage vs. Protection measures: the growing disconnect"; research.att.com.
www2.research.att.com/~bala/papers/w2sp11.pdf

"Prepared Statement of the Federal Trade Commission on Consumer Privacy and Protection in the Mobile Marketplace"; Senate Committee on Commerce, Science, and Transportation, May 19, 2001.
www.ftc.gov/os/testimony/110519mobilemarketplace.pdf

"Protecting Consumer Privacy in an Era of Rapid Change"; FTC Staff Report.
www.ftc.gov/os/2010/12/101201privacyreport.pdf

"Preliminary FTC Staff Privacy Report: Remarks of Chairman
Jon Leibowitz"; December 2, 2010.
www.ftc.gov/speeches/leibowitz/101201privacyreportremarks.pdf

"Data Mining: How Companies Now Know Everything About You";
time.com, March 10, 2011.
www.time.com/time/magazine/article/0,9171,2058205,00.html

"An Empirical Study of Privacy-Violating Information Flows in JavaScript
Web Applications"; Dongseok Jang, Ranjit Jhala, Sorin Lerner,
Hovav Shacham at the University of California, San Diego.
http://cseweb.ucsd.edu/~d1jang/papers/ccs10.pdf

"Stanford students create 'do not track' software"; Stanford.edu, December 2, 2010.
http://news.stanford.edu/news/2010/december/do-not-track-120210.html

"'Dating' site imports 250,000 Facebook profiles without permission;
cnn.com, February 4, 2011.
www.cnn.com/2011/TECH/social.media/02/04/dating.site.facebook.
wired/index.html

"Sens. Franken, Schumer, Whitehouse, Blumenthal Warn New Facebook Plan
May Reveal Sensitive User Information, Increasing Risk For Fraud, Theft
And Abuse"; franken.senate.gov, March 9, 2011.
www.franken.senate.gov/?p=press_release&id=1374

"Do Not Track Isn't Just About Behavorial Advertising";
cyberlaw.standford.edu, December 20, 2010.
http://cyberlaw.stanford.edu/node/6573

"Mozilla's Comments in Response to the FTC's Inquiry on Privacy";
blog.mozilla.org, March 2, 2011.
http://blog.mozilla.org/blog/2011/03/02/mozillas-comments-in-response-
to-the-ftcs-inquiry-on-privacy

"Why 'Anonymous' Data Sometimes Isn't"; schneier.com, December 13, 2007.
www.schneier.com/essay-200.html

"A Face Is Exposed for AOL Searcher No. 4417749"; nytimes.com, August 9, 2006.
www.nytimes.com/2006/08/09/technology/09aol.html?_r=1&ex=13127760
00&en=f6f61949c6da4d38&ei=5090

"Anonymous Emails Can Be Traced to Authors, Concordia U. Research Shows"; chronicle.com, March 10, 2011.
http://chronicle.com/blogs/wiredcampus/anonymous-emails-can-be-traced-to-authors-concordia-u-research-shows/30264

Privacy in Peril: How We Are Sacrificing a Fundamental Right in Exchange for Security and Convenience. James B. Rule. Oxford University Press, 2009. 978-0195394368

"The Promise and Peril of Big Data"; The Aspen Institute.
www.aspeninstitute.org/publications/promise-peril-big-data

"How Companies Learn Your Secrets"; nytimes.com, February 16, 2012.
www.nytimes.com/2012/02/19/magazine/shopping-habits.html

"Updating our privacy policies and terms of service"; googleblog.blogspot.com, January 24, 2012.
http://googleblog.blogspot.com/2012/01/updating-our-privacy-policies-and-terms.html

"Public Or Private: Keeping Google From Being 'Evil'"; npr.org, January 29, 2012.
www.npr.org/2012/01/29/146062607/public-or-private-keeping-google-from-being-evil

"E.U. Presses Google to Delay Privacy Policy Changes"; nytimes.com, February 3, 2012.
www.nytimes.com/2012/02/04/technology/eu-backs-delay-in-googles-privacy-policy.html

CHAPTER 6: YOUR MONEY

"The Conscience of a Hacker"; phrack.org, written January 8, 1986.
www.phrack.org/issues.html?issue=7&id=3&mode=txt

"Steve Jackson Games v. Secret Service Case Archive"; eff.org.
https://w2.eff.org/legal/cases/SJG

"TJX Hacker Charged With Heartland, Hannaford Breaches"; wired.com, August 17, 2009.
www.wired.com/threatlevel/2009/08/tjx-hacker-charged-with-heartland

"Breach Brings Scrutiny"; wsj.com, April 5, 2011.
http://online.wsj.com/article/SB10001424052748704587004576245131531712342.html

NOTES

"Citigroup Sued by Cardholders Over May Security Breach"; bloomberg.com, October 7, 2011.
www.bloomberg.com/news/2011-10-07/citigroup-sued-in-n-y-by-cardholders-over-security-breaches.html

"Who falls for phish?: a demographic analysis of phishing susceptibility and effectiveness of interventions"; acm.org.
http://dl.acm.org/citation.cfm?id=1753383

"In Internet stickups, consumers risk being left on their own"; nytimes.com, February 16, 2005.
www.nytimes.com/2005/02/15/technology/15iht-netbank.html

"Florida man sues bank over $90K wire fraud"; theregister.co.uk, February 8, 2005.
www.theregister.co.uk/2005/02/08/e-banking_trojan_lawsuit

"ZeuS on the Hunt"; securelist.com.
www.securelist.com/en/analysis/204792107/ZeuS_on_the_Hunt

"FBI: Crime Ring Stole $70 Million Using Computer Virus"; abcnews.go.com, October 1, 2010.
http://abcnews.go.com/Blotter/fbi-crime-ring-stole-70-million-computer-virus/story?id=11777873

LulzSec material dump, June 25, 2011.
http://pastebin.com/1znEGmHa

LulzSec Twitter status update, June 13, 2011, 9:57 am.
https://twitter.com/LulzSec/statuses/80317828338679810

"LulzSec disbands: Final cache includes AT&T internal data and 750,000 user accounts"; zdnet.com, June 25, 2011.
www.zdnet.com/blog/igeneration/lulzsec-disbands-final-cache-includes-at-t-internal-data-and-750000-user-accounts/11134

"Lulzsec fiasco"; blog.hidemyass.com, September 23, 2011.
http://blog.hidemyass.com/2011/09/23/lulzsec-fiasco

"Cybercrime Outlook 2020" Kaspersky Lab.
www.kaspersky.com/about/news/virus/2011/Cybercrime_Outlook_2020_From_Kaspersky_Lab

"Cyber security by the numbers: Malware surges, spam declines in third quarter"; zdnet.com, November 17, 2010.
www.zdnet.com/blog/btl/cyber-security-by-the-numbers-malware-surges-spam-declines-in-third-quarter/41818

"FTC Releases List of Top Consumer Complaints in 2010; Identity Theft Tops the List Again"; ftc.gov, March 8, 2011.
www.ftc.gov/opa/2011/03/topcomplaints.shtm

"GpCode-like Ransomware Is Back"; securelist.com, November 29, 2010.
www.securelist.com/en/blog/333/GpCode_like_Ransomware_Is_Back

"Ohio State notifies of unauthorized access to university server"; osu.edu, December 15, 2010.
www.osu.edu/news/newsitem2985

The Hacker Crackdown: Law and Disorder on the Electronic Frontier. Bruce Sterling. Bantam, 1993. 978-0553563702

"Nigerian Fraud Scams"; consumer.georgia.gov.
http://consumer.georgia.gov/consumer-topics/nigerian-fraud-scams

"A Culture of Corruption: Everyday Deception and Popular Discontent in Nigeria"; press.princeton.edu.
http://press.princeton.edu/titles/8266.html

"FBI Underboss Says Cyber Criminals the New Mafia"; esecurityplanet.com, March 23, 2010.
www.esecurityplanet.com/trends/article.php/3872326/FBI-Underboss-Says-Cyber-Criminals-the-New-Mafia.htm

"eMicrosoft Leads Zeus Botnet Server Shutdown"; informationweek.com, March 26, 2012.
www.informationweek.com/news/security/attacks/232700229

"Microsoft raid targets cyber Mafia intel"; cnn.com, March 26, 2012.
http://money.cnn.com/2012/03/26/technology/microsoft-raid/index.htm

"Zeus Trojan hits Android smartphones"; msnbc.msn.com, July 12, 2011.
www.msnbc.msn.com/id/43728379/ns/technology_and_science-wireless/t/zeus-trojan-hits-android-smartphones

NOTES

"Zeus Variant Using Fake Cash-Back & Fraud Protection Offers to Steal Debit Card Information"; hyphenet.com, May 18, 2012.
www.hyphenet.com/blog/2012/05/18/zeus-variant-using-fake-cash-back-fraud-protection-offers-to-steal-debit-card-information

"Zeus Trojan Spreading via Facebook Friend Requests"; infosecisland.com, August 24, 2011.
www.infosecisland.com/blogview/16077-Zeus-Trojan-Spreading-via-Facebook-Friend-Requests.html

"LulzSec hacker Sabu leads FBI to others, arrests"; latimes.com, March 6, 2012.
http://articles.latimes.com/2012/mar/06/business/la-fi-tn-alleged-lulzsec-hackers-arrested-20120306

"Arrests Sow Mistrust Inside a Clan of Hackers"; nytimes.com, March 6, 2012.
www.nytimes.com/2012/03/07/technology/lulzsec-hacking-suspects-are-arrested.html

"Was our interview with LulzSec hacker an FBI set-up?"; newscientist.com, March 14, 2012.
www.newscientist.com/article/mg21328566.300-was-our-interview-with-lulzsec-hacker-an-fbi-setup.html

"Hacker Sabu Worked Nonstop As Government Informer"; informationweek.com, March 9, 2012.
www.informationweek.com/news/security/vulnerabilities/232602334

CHAPTER 7: YOUR DNA

"What's 23andMe Really Selling? (Cuz the Feds Are Asking.)"; motherjones.com, May 20, 2010.
www.motherjones.com/mojo/2010/05/23andme-navigenetics-pathway-genomics-henry-waxman-investigation

"Patenting and Personal Genomics: 23andMe Receives its First Patent, and Plenty of Questions"; genomicslawreport.com, June 1, 2012.
www.genomicslawreport.com/index.php/2012/06/01/patenting-and-personal-genomics-23andme-receives-its-first-patent-and-plenty-of-questions

"Commission Sues Railroad To End Genetic Testing In Work Injury Cases"; nytimes.com, February 10, 2001.
www.nytimes.com/2001/02/10/us/commission-sues-railroad-to-end-genetic-testing-in-work-injury-cases.html

"EEOC AND BNSF SETTLE GENETIC TESTING CASE UNDER AMERI-CANS WITH DISABILITIES ACT"; eeoc.gov, May 8, 2002.
www.eeoc.gov/eeoc/newsroom/release/5-8-02.cfm

"Testimony of Mr. Gary Avary, Member of the Brotherhood of Maintenance of Way Employes and Employee of Burlington Northern Santa Fe Railroad Company", House Subcommittee on Employer-Employee Relations, July 24, 2001.
http://archives.republicans.edlabor.house.gov/archive/hearings/107th/eer/genetic72401/avary.htm

"The Book of Life: How the Completion of the Human Genome Project was Revealed to the Public"; hea.sagepub.com.
http://hea.sagepub.com/content/6/4/445.abstract

"How To Break Anonymity of the Netflix Prize Dataset"; Cornell University Library (arxiv.org), October 18, 2006.
http://arxiv.org/abs/cs/0610105

"'Anonymized' data really isn't—and here's why not"; arstechnica.com, September 8, 2009.
http://arstechnica.com/tech-policy/2009/09/your-secrets-live-online-in-databases-of-ruin

"Chronology of Data Breaches: Security Breaches 2005 – Present"; privacyrights.org, updated June 13, 2012.
www.privacyrights.org/data-breach

"Trustworthy Designs for the Nationwide Health Information Network: Privacy Commentary"; dataprivacylab.org.
http://dataprivacylab.org/projects/nhin3/index.html

"A sensible censor for sharing medical records"; web.mit.edu, July 23, 2008.
http://web.mit.edu/newsoffice/2008/robo-censor-0723.html

"World Privacy Forum Consumer Advisory: The Potential Privacy Risks in Personal Health Records Every Consumer Needs to Know About"; World Privacy Forum, February 20, 2008.
www.worldprivacyforum.org/pdf/WPF_PHRConsumerAdvisory_02_20_2008fs.pdf

"Sorrell vs. IMS Health, Inc."; scotusblog.com, June 23, 2011.
www.scotusblog.com/case-files/cases/sorrell-v-ims-health-inc?wpmp_switcher=desktop

"Sorrell v. IMS Health"; eff.org, March 1, 2011.
www.eff.org/cases/sorrell-v-ims-health

"What Information is "Personally Identifiable"?"; eff.org, September 11, 2009.
www.eff.org/deeplinks/2009/09/what-information-personally-identifiable

"Our data, ourselves"; boston.com, May 22, 2011.
www.boston.com/bostonglobe/ideas/articles/2011/05/22/our_data_ourselves

"HealthVault breaks free from the desktop!"; blogs.msdn.com, May 31, 2011.
http://blogs.msdn.com/b/familyhealthguy/archive/2011/05/31/healthvault-breaks-free-from-the-desktop.aspx

CHAPTER 8: YOUR KIDS
"Leveson inquiry: phone hacking 'made Dowlers think Milly was alive'";
guardian.co.uk, November 21, 2011.
www.guardian.co.uk/media/2011/nov/21/leveson-inquiry-phone-hacking-dowlers

"Corrections and clarifications: News of the World and Milly Dowler";
guardian.co.uk, December 20, 2011.
www.guardian.co.uk/theguardian/2011/dec/20/corrections-and-clarifications

"Your child is safe. But is his identity? Find out with a Free
ChildScan Report"; allclearid.
www.allclearid.com/child

"Reading, Writing, and RFID Chips: A Scary Back-to-School Future in
California"; eff.org, August 30, 2010.
www.eff.org/deeplinks/2010/08/reading-writing-and-rfid-chips-scary-back-school

"Tracking Teen Drivers: The Latest Tech To Keep Tabs on Your Kids";
edmunds.com, July 7, 2009.
www.edmunds.com/car-technology/tracking-teen-drivers.
html?articleid=152146

"Privacy and Publicity in the Context of Big Data"; danah.org, April 29, 2010.
www.danah.org/papers/talks/2010/WWW2010.html

"Rise In Child Identity Theft Prompts Push For Solutions";
huffingtonpost.com, December 21, 2011.
www.huffingtonpost.com/news/burdened-beginnings

"Family Secrets: Parents Prey On Children's Identities As Victims Stay Silent";
huffingtonpost.com, December 11, 2011.
www.huffingtonpost.com/2011/11/11/child-identity-theft-parents-credit-
fraud-debt_n_1010093.html

"James Murdoch Steps Down From British Broadcaster"; nytimes.com, April 3, 2012.
www.nytimes.com/2012/04/04/world/europe/james-murdoch-steps-
down-from-british-broadcaster.html

"Secret Service interrogates 13-year-old over Facebook post";
today.msnbc.msn.com, May 18, 2011.
http://digitallife.today.msnbc.msn.com/_news/2011/05/18/6667233-secret-
service-interrogates-13-year-old-over-facebook-post?lite

"Outrage as Girl Is Suspended From School Over Bin Laden Facebook Post";
foxnews.com, May 19, 2011.
www.foxnews.com/us/2011/05/19/outrage-girl-suspended-school-bin-
laden-facebook-post

"Student Suspended for Facebook Post"; mhsmirador.com, February 4, 2011.
www.mhsmirador.com/news/2011/02/04/student-suspended-for-facebook-post

"Facebook prank costs 4 Stillwater girls hockey players a game";
youth1st.com, February 10, 2011.
www.youth1st.com/blog/87-facebook-prank-costs-4-stillwater-girls-
hockey-players-a-game

"Student off hook for Facebook insult of teacher"; sfgate.com, January 29, 2011.
www.wvec.com/my-city/chesapeake/Chesapeake-student-suspended-for-
threatening-post-on-Facebook-133365228.html

"Students suspended, expelled over Facebook posts"; zdnet.com, March 4, 2011.
www.zdnet.com/blog/facebook/students-suspended-expelled-over-facebook-posts/517

"Girl who faces stalking charge after Facebook post says deputy went too far";
tampabay.com, December 30, 2011.
www.tampabay.com/news/education/k12/article1208333.ece

"Labor: Demanding applicants' social media passwords may open the door to
discrimination claims"; insidecounsel.com, April 2, 2012.
www.insidecounsel.com/2012/04/02/labor-demanding-applicants-social-
media-passwords

"Google and the Search for the Future"; wsj.com, August 14, 2010.
http://online.wsj.com/article/SB10001424052748704901104575423294099527212.html

CHAPTER 9: DEFENDING YOUR IDENTITY

"Timeline: A History of Privacy in America"; scientificamerican.com, September 5, 2008.
www.scientificamerican.com/article.cfm?id=timeline-a-history-of-privacy

"Four Ways to Fight Back Against Cyber Attacks"; popularmechanics.com,
October 1, 2009.
www.popularmechanics.com/technology/gadgets/news/4295130

"When Hackers Attack: Practicing Cybersecurity at Home";
popularmechanics.com, October 1, 2009.
www.popularmechanics.com/technology/gadgets/news/4295100

"IE9 and Privacy: Introducing Tracking Protection"; blogs.msdn.com, December 7, 2010.
http://blogs.msdn.com/b/ie/archive/2010/12/07/ie9-and-privacy-introduc-
ing-tracking-protection-v8.aspx

"Botnet Detection"; shadowserver.org.
www.shadowserver.org/wiki/pmwiki.php/Information/BotnetDetection

"New privacy feature in Hotmail allows use of multiple email aliases";
technet.com, February 4, 2011.
http://blogs.technet.com/b/privacyimperative/archive/2011/02/04/new-
privacy-feature-in-hotmail-allows-use-of-multiple-email-aliases.aspx

"Apple Loophole Gives Developers Access to Photos"; blogs.nytimes.com,
February 28, 2012.
http://bits.blogs.nytimes.com/2012/02/28/tk-ios-gives-developers-access-
to-photos-videos-location

"Symantec Smartphone Honey Stick Project"; Symantec.com.
www.symantec.com/about/news/resources/press_kits/detail.
jsp?pkid=symantec-smartphone-honey-stick-project

"Mac Flashback malware: What it is and how to get rid of it (FAQ)";
cnet.com, April 5, 2012.
http://news.cnet.com/8301-27076_3-57410050-248/mac-flashback-mal-
ware-what-it-is-and-how-to-get-rid-of-it-faq

"FBI makes arrest after Johansson, Aguilera emails hacked"; cnn.com, October 12, 2011.
http://articles.cnn.com/2011-10-12/entertainment/showbiz_hacking-
arrest_1_mails-authorities-charge-identity-theft?_s=PM:SHOWBIZ

"Michigan Teacher's Aide Said She Was Disciplined for Not Giving Boss Facebook Access"; abcnews.go.com, April 3, 2012. http://abcnews.go.com/Business/michigan-teacher-disciplined-providing-access-facebook-page/story?id=16056231

"More information than you ever wanted: does Facebook bring out the green-eyed monster of jealousy?"; ncbi.nlm.nih.gov, August 2009. www.ncbi.nlm.nih.gov/pubmed/19366318

FURTHER RESOURCES

DOWNLOADS
Tor (available for multiple operating systems)
www.torproject.org/download/download

PrivacyMark (various browsers)
www.privacychoice.org/privacymark

PrivacyChoice Opt Out extension (Chrome-only, for now)
www.privacychoice.org/trackerblock/chrome

IP ADDRESS INFORMATION
What's My IP Address:
http://whatismyipaddress.com

IP-related Information
www.whatsmyip.org/more

SECURITY THREAT NOTIFICATION
Internet Storm Center: Regularly updated bulletin of new security threats
http://isc.sans.edu

Norton Cybercrime Index: Quick, stock-exchange-like gauge of current
cybercrime threat level (available on Norton 360 software)
http://us.norton.com/360

Privacy Clearinghouse's Chronology of Data Breaches: Searchable database
of reported data breaches
www.privacyrights.org/data-breach

Dataloss db's Breach Database
http://datalossdb.org

FTC's Identity Theft Site
www.ftc.gov/idtheft

INDEX

ABOUT THE AUTHORS

ERIK SOFGE is a journalist who covers science, technology and culture. He is a contributing editor at *Popular Mechanics*, and his work has also appeared in *Men's Journal*, *Slate*, the *Wall Street Journal*, and the 2012 edition of the *Best American Science Writing* anthology series. Call it bravery, or stupidity, but despite having had various accounts compromised by hackers over the years, as well as his identity stolen, the old-fashioned way—with checks that were physically intercepted and cashed illicitly—he has yet to put a password on his wireless router, or purchase one of those fancy, lockable mailboxes. He lives with his wife and daughter in Massachusetts.

DAVIN COBURN is a senior contributor at *Popular Mechanics* magazine. He has covered science, technology and adventure for the magazine for the past eight years, and served on the *Popular Mechanics* team that conducted groundbreaking research into debunking 9/11 conspiracy theories. His work has also appeared in *Men's Journal*, *Private Air*, *Islands*, *National Geographic Traveler*, and newspapers across the country. He lives in Brooklyn, New York.